HOW YOU FOUND ME

Cienna Collins

Copyright © 2024 Cienna Collins

All rights reserved. No part of this publication may be reproduced, stored in or introduced into a retrieval system, or transmitted, in any form, or by any means (electronic, mechanical, photocopying, recording, or otherwise) without the prior written permission of the copyright owner of this book.

This is a work of fiction. Names, characters, places, businesses, services, brands, media and incidents are either the product of the author's imagination or are used fictitiously.

AJC Publishing
PO Box 8050
Oakleigh East Vic 3166 Australia
E: aj@ajcpublishing.com.au
W: www.ajcpublishing.com.au

ISBN:
978-1-7637190-5-7 Print
978-1-7637190-6-4 Ebook
978-0-9954140-7-5 Audiobook

Interior design by AJC Publishing
Cover design by GetCovers
Image licensing: Depositphotos
Typeset in EB Garamond 12
Printed and bound by IngramSpark
Edition 2 published 2024
Edition 1 published 2020 as Oleanders Are Poisonous by AJ Collins

Also by Cienna Collins

How You Left Me (Part 1)
How You Found Me (Part 2)
The Disappearing Season

Praise for How You Found Me

Collins expertly guides us through Lauren's brutal, complicated coming of age in a poignant tale about growing up too fast, forgiving too slowly, and the healing power of love, friendship, and family – however it comes.
- *Nicole Hayes, author of The Whole of My World, One True thing and A Shadow's Breath*

Hard to put down, this is a nuanced and entertaining coming of age tale. Collins sheds light on the dark experiences of life and delves into the hope and security that is borne of connection. With empathy and insight, Collins reveals the power of vulnerability and the importance of finding your tribe. A big-hearted novel about love and trust. About when to let go, and when to hold on.
- *Melissa Manning, author of Smokehouse Collection*

Author's Note

Content warning: References to sexual abuse, mental health, suicide, self-harm, homophobia.

Grammar note: This book uses Australian spelling and grammar conventions.

From the author: While I have experienced some of the issues explored in this work, the character of Lauren is not me. All the characters depicted in this book are fictional. The story is, however, based on a kernel of murky truth, which has lain simmering within me for years, and like the stone within Lauren, it needed to see daylight.

I hope that each of my books will entertain and move you, that each is an act of escapism, a moment to step away from your everyday life, pause and introspect.

For My Chickens
For the magic of friendship

Vulnerability is a journey to destiny

One stole her innocence
One stole her heart
One gave her hope
And the secret awoke

1

Excruciating

Bad things happen on my birthdays. Like this boozy mob. They look as though they're enjoying a lynching: mine. Talk about sweating it. Whoever invented the karaoke machine must have had ancestors who cheered at public executions, back when Marie Antoinette fictitiously told everyone to eat cake. I'm supposed to be geeing-up this Fitzroy pub crowd, not that they need it.

Oh god. It might seem as though I'm pulling a dance move, but I'm just trying to avoid getting my heels caught in the gap between the stage risers. With each shift, I have to peel the soles of my boots off the sticky carpet.

I'm staring at lyrics that make me think Justin Bieber and Rihanna are conspiring to give birth to a love child: baby, baby, baby; yeah, yeah, yeah; give it to me, give it to me. The poor excuse for a song breaks into a rap section, and I stand with one hand in my jeans pocket, a dork waiting for the torture to end.

Bob picked the song. "The punters'll go for it," he said.

They're not. They're holding their beers aloft, laughing at my piss-poor effort to get the party started. My face is burning, and it's not from the fuggy heat of the bar. It's because I can sing. Properly. Just not this rubbish. Let me die. Now.

It's a vocal limp to the end of the track before I shove the microphone back onto the stand. Bob collects several scraps of paper – scribbled song requests from Elvis and Beyoncé wannabes who think they can do a better job than me. Yeah, everyone can sing when they're drunk. He lumbers onto the stage. "Give it up for Lauren, our very own Rihanna!" The applause is surprisingly enthusiastic, but I'm sure it's more about getting me off the stage. I'm seriously happy to comply.

Safe behind the bar, I wrap my apron around my waist. It's back to pulling beers, cracking UDLs and batting off puns based on my crap performance. Suddenly, it's comedy hour:

"Hey, love. you should eat more tuna! Get it? Tune-er?"

"I'll tune her if she likes!"

Hilarious. As I bend to the lower fridge to grab a pear cider for the chick in the tight skirt and even tighter t-shirt, some dickhead throws a bottle top at my butt. I spring upright, lean across the bar and threaten him with the prong of a corkscrew.

"Not cool," I hiss.

The guy holds both hands up, claiming innocence while his mate beside him guffaws. In the seconds it takes me to realise I've chosen the wrong perpetrator, guffawing guy's shoulder is grasped by a tall blond dude.

"Apologise," the dude says.

"Sorry, love."

I'm thrown, unsure whether to tell the blond dude thanks very much, but I can look after myself, or to smile my gratitude. I choose grateful. Decency is rare in this bar. Heckle and Jeckle take their beers elsewhere while the dude sits at the bar.

"Hey, birthday girl."

I swear my heart stops for a second. No-one but Snap knows it's my birthday, that I'm finally legal. I look closer and recognition hits me: the grey eyes, the wide smile, the face – now hidden behind a mass of hipster beard. His hair is longer and tied back in a loose ponytail.

"Spell serendipitous," he says.

"Harry?"

For a second, I have this insane reflex to turn and run.

2

Ambivalence

Harry's talking over the noise of the karaoke, and I have to focus to hear above all the memories and apprehensions clamouring for my brain's attention. I'm like a goldfish, all mouth popping and no words.

"How did you find me?"

"Pure luck." He grins. All white teeth and charisma.

"Uh huh." I'm not sure I believe him. And I'm not sure how I feel about him finding me.

"It must be a relief to be legal at last," he says.

I panic. Flash him a look.

"Just teasing."

A girl two seats away bleats at me, "Hey! Are you serving tonight or what?"

I tell her to chill her bits and ask Harry what he'd like. He orders boutique, of course. What else would he drink in his designer-looking suit? And since when did Harry wear suits? His white shirt emphasises what smooth, tanned skin is visible on his face. That beard. I don't like it.

He sips on the frothing neck, then looks directly at me. "You should be singing Adele. Or something classier." He follows this with a killer smile that sends me back to that porch, his guitar, the hammock. Home.

"Yeah, right."

I fetch the girl her Cruiser and come back to Harry. I want to know why he's here. How he found me. And does anyone else know?

"You still sound good. Up there." He nods towards the stage

"Ha. I only do it cos the boss insists."

"You always did underestimate yourself. You're looking great, by the way. Grown up nice."

"Thanks." I grin, chuffed even though it's probably a line. Snap's taught me to recognise them. I've also picked up that giving an indulgent smile, big eyes and a blank expression leads to bigger tips. The guys like it. A lot. But this is Harry.

I pour a fifth – or is it a sixth? – bourbon and Coke for the ginger-bearded bloke next to him. "Last one for a while," I tell Ginger, with an I'm-not-to-blame, I'm-just-the-help look. He smiles and holds his glass up. "Cheers." He'll be back in half an hour asking for another.

I glance at Harry. I'm not going to do polite conversation. "So, what are you doing here?"

"I came to hear you sing again."

"What?"

"I heard you last week."

I gape. He was here and didn't say anything? How did I miss that? I face him, hands on hips. "That's a little creepy."

He shrugs. "Ever considered going pro?"

"Yeah, sure. All the time." I slosh a glass into a tub of soapy water, ready for the dishwasher.

This is too weird. I haven't seen him in, what, over two years, and this is the conversation?

"Listen, I'm serious. If you're interested..." He reaches into his pocket.

Who is he kidding? I'm too short, too awkward, too ordinary, and not dumb enough to fall for it. Professional singers are skinny chicks with amazing voices and the confidence to wear anything, anytime and get away with it. On a kind day, when I haven't consumed a whole jar of Nutella, I'd call myself curvy. But it's not just that. Picking up where we left off would be taking a huge step backwards. I left Wineera to forget.

A Roy Orbison backing track starts up, and there's raucous cheering and clapping for some regular who always picks "Blue Bayou" and "Pretty Woman". Harry is distracted, writing something on the paper he's pulled from his pocket. I move further down the bar to clear empties from the beer mat. I can't help glancing back. He's hot. He looks up from his writing and catches me peeking. He smiles, too wide, too white, too perfect. I melt, and for sure I'm blushing. This is not good. I have to escape. Somewhere. Anywhere.

With a tilt of my head, I signal to Snap. "Smoko." Not that I smoke, but it's the only legitimate way to get a break apart from a flying toilet visit. Snap has a cocktail shaker in mid-flight. He flutters a hand at me and yells over the din of the karaoke.

"Take your time, honey. I've got you covered."

As I pass Harry, I lean over and shout, "Taking a break. Great to see you." I don't wait for a reply.

The loading dock stinks with its industrial bins, but it's the only quiet place for a minute's peace. I sit in a ratty chair, careful to avoid the filthy card table with its overflowing ashtray.

Hell. Harry.

I lean back and take in the night sky. It's clear, though the city lights are obliterating billions of stars. That's something to be said for back home. If you take away the stuff you don't want to remember, the Mallee has a beauty, a quality that words alone can't capture. Something gets imprinted in you.

And great. Now I'm thinking about Mum, and that sets off the guilts because I've never been back. Not that she'd recognise me in her state. I do call the hospice now and then though – only from the pub's payphone, in case I get traced. It's paranoia, but there was the fire, and ... I can't be dragged back to that life. I just can't.

The nurses say Mum's doing okay but deteriorating, which is normal. It must be awful being so dependent, unable to communicate, even to ask for a simple glass of water. I sometimes wonder if euthanasia became legal, would I be capable of helping her along? And would I know if she was ready to die? Too hard basket.

Damn Harry for bringing it all back. What's he really doing here anyway? I sigh. It's incredibly rude to avoid him like this, but I don't know what to say to him. Wineera seems like another lifetime. He better not tell anyone he's found me.

The noise from inside rises a level as Bob opens the back door and sticks his head through the tangle of flyscreen tassels. "Hey! What're you doin'?"

I hold up my water bottle. "Just getting some air. I'll be there in a mini. Gotta go to the loo."

"Move a bit faster, will you? Drinks don't serve themselves."

When he turns his back, I pull a face and give him the bird. It took me only one night to figure out I don't like Bob. Eight months on has made no improvement. He's relentless. "Why don't you wear a skirt, sweetie? You'll get bigger tips."

I've told him not to call me "Sweetie" or "Honey". It makes me want to retch. Snap, on the other hand, still calls me Kitten, and I don't mind. He's affectionate; Bob's a perv.

I'm not sure what's worse: the early hours and minimum wage at my old supermarket job, or the drunken fools and stench of stale alcohol here. At least there's Snap. It doesn't matter anyway, because soon we're both going to restart our VCE, then I'll get a better part-time job when I start uni. Not sure what I'll aim for yet. Maybe primary school teaching. Or kindy. Little kids are cool. They don't bullshit. There's a childcare centre I pass on my way to work here. I love seeing all those rosy faces, curly heads and cute backpacks. What's not to like?

Anyhow, as long as Bob keeps his hands to himself, I can put up with this place.

Sigh. Time to head back into the fray. I pause behind the flyscreen tassels. Bob has the freakin' things everywhere. They're usually annoying, catching on our food trays, but tonight they're earning their keep as camouflage while I check if Harry has gone.

Damn. He's still there, handing something to Snap. Snap gives him a wink and a salute. "Yes, sir!" he sing-songs. Harry turns and leaves. Good, now I can relax. I take my position at the bar and eye Snap. He's busy writing something.

When he's done, he slinks over and makes a production of handing me a folded note. I love how he feels free to be himself here. He's like a dancer the way he moves, sleek as a cat.

I ignore his outstretched paw. "You auditioning for Strictly Ballroom?"

"Biartch! And here I am doing you a favour." He bumps me with his hip. "He wants to buy you a birthday drink."

I shake my head. "No."

"Just take it, honey. He can probably throw you a better party than I can."

"I told you, I don't want a party."

"Sheesh! When was the last time, anyway? I bet it's like the Sahara down there."

I ignore him, turning to a customer. Snap moves behind me and shoves the note in the back pocket of my jeans. Anyone else, I would have biffed them, but Snap is the closest thing to a sister I've ever had. He'd love me for saying that.

"Call him," Snap says. "If you don't, I will."

"Yeah, maybe."

"Maybe won't get the lady laid."

"You do know we both went to school with him?"

"What?" He puts his hand over his heart. "I missed my opportunity? Who is he?"

"Harry Carter. We used to be study buddies."

"Well! Second time around is even better."

"We never... we're not even..."

"One word," he says. "Fuck buddies."

"Snap!" I fake a shocked look. "That's two words. And wash your mouth out. It's not going to happen."

Snap slaps my butt and saunters off to stack glasses in the bench-top dishwasher. I can't help grinning; he's a brilliant human being. And he knows I love him – he tells me so all the time. I can imagine what would happen if I brought Harry home to meet him: sly looks, offerings of scrambled eggs in bed in the morning, jokes about threesomes. And worse – our apartment building might be brick on the outside, but the wall between our bedrooms is only plasterboard. Anyone I dared to share my bed with would get an eye-opening education in the thin hours of the morning. That's when Snap starts working his phone-sex line.

He says most clients are lonely guys who are happy to rack up a quick few minutes talking dirty before finishing, but his ultimate favourite is the rare female who sits on the line for up to forty-five minutes while he builds up her self-esteem. He says someone has to provide the service to those in need.

Who am I to judge? It helps pay his share of the rent.

"Earth to planet Lauren." Snap is clicking his fingers at me. "Thinking about Mr Hunkarama?"

"No. I just remembered our rent is due tomorrow."

He makes a pouty face. "Killjoy."

We both turn our heads as a barrage of squealing girls bursts into the bar, complete with a hen in frilly white veil and pink sash declaring her the Bride-to-Be.

"Oh goodie," Snap sighs. "It's Katy Perry and her entourage."

Bob has come behind the bar to top up his drink, but he hurries back to the stage, starts up the karaoke machine and yells, "Ladies and gentlemen, please welcome our very own Meghan Trainor." He points at me. I roll my eyes and head up to the stage where Bob throws me the mic. It smells like beer. God, it's nearly one in the morning, and I wish I were in bed. As I sing "Dear future husband" I look around the bar. Which spot was Harry hiding in last week when I missed him?

3

Irreparable

It's afternoon, and I'm squatting at a low shelf in the storage room, loading up with limes to stock the bar. Prepping is like therapy for me: time to centre myself before the crowds filter in after five. I slice lemons and limes into fine half-moons, lining them up like fallen dominos on a tray, ready to pinch into bottles of boutique beer, or slip into fizzing gin and tonics. Half strawberries, dipped in castor sugar, and little pineapple chunks sit on a separate tray. That's as far as we go here – no paper umbrellas.

Normally, my mind is a blank, relaxed, but for the past five days there's been something niggling me: Harry. I keep expecting him to show up again. To settle at the bar, wanting to reminisce about old times. "Do you remember that ram in the back paddock? The time we forgot to shut the gate, and he got into the garden and ate all that clover, then blew up like a balloon and Dad nearly killed me? Or what about when you snuck over to my place when you were supposed to be studying and your bike got a flat tyre, and you had to push it all the way home, and Samuel went off his rocker?"

Samuel. Why did I have to think of him? That life is dead. Buried. Literally. I shake it off. It's Harry's fault. Why did he have to turn up? And the bigger question is, why hasn't he been back to ask me about the fire? I can't help but wonder if he's dobbed me in. Surely not. Surely the police would have turned up by now?

As I stand and straighten, I bump into Bob who's on his way out back for a ciggie.

"Careful, love."

"Sorry, boss."

He stands there regarding me. "You know, I can't figure why you won't listen to me. Here." He sticks his unlit cigarette in his mouth and steps forward. Before I know it, he's popped my top two buttons and pulled my blouse open halfway down my chest, revealing my bra.

I'm dumb with shock.

"There," he says, flattening out my collar. "Much better. Bit of cleavage. You watch. Your tip jar'll double tonight."

Suddenly limes are thudding all over the floor, and my hand is stinging from the slap I've landed on Bob's face.

"Fuck!" he says, stunned. He reaches to pluck his crushed cigarette from his mouth. "What was that for?"

"You're a moron!" I snatch my shirt together, turn and scramble through the plastic strips that separate the storeroom from the bar. My arm catches in a tangle, and I yank hard, tearing half the strips from their mooring. Snap has just arrived. He looks startled.

"Kitten? What's happened? You okay?"

"Enough's enough," I mutter, ripping off my apron. "I quit." I grab my bag from underneath the counter.

"What's he done?"

"Broke the camel's back." I try to push past Snap, but he blocks me.

"Honey, slow down. Tell me what happened."

I glare at him. "Get out of my way."

He looks unsure, but finally says, "Do you want me to drive you home?"

"No."

"Well, if you're going to go ..." he reaches up to the top shelf and takes down a bottle of Famous Grouse thirty-year-old scotch, "you should go out with a bang."

"I can't take that. It's worth a fortune."

"Sure you can. You're never going to get your back wages out of him. So shhh." He shoves it in my bag. "Go."

I round the bar and continue through to the bistro, where the only patrons – a couple of grey-haired veterans who spend their pensions sucking on pints all afternoon, every afternoon – glance at me, then return their gaze to the sports channel on the overhead telly.

"Give us a top-up would ya, love?" one says, holding out an empty beer jug. I pause for a moment, then take the jug from him, pull the scotch out of my bag and stick it into his hand. "Merry Christmas."

The veterans' cries of surprise are cut off as the door swings shut behind me. Out on the street, I lean back against the brickwork of the pub, bag clutched to my stomach, waiting for my shaking to subside. A couple of tradies in shorts are approaching. One stubs a cigarette on the footpath with his Blundstone while the other, the one wearing a grubby singlet, looks me over. He seems about to speak before his mate pushes him through the door and into the pub.

The bistro will be filling soon – punters wanting their Wednesday night Ten-Dollar-Parmas. Bob will be swearing at being short-staffed. Good. He should have thought of that before he put his disgusting hands on me.

As I move to heft my bag over my shoulder, I notice my bra is still showing, the white satin stark against the black of my shirt. I button up properly, wondering if that's what caused the singlet bloke to stare at me. Creep.

A little calmer now, I wander off towards a music store two blocks away. I can't afford to buy anything, especially now, but I don't feel like going home yet. I need to walk. To think. I've screwed up. Snap's going to have to cover my half of the rent now. And I was just starting to get ahead with a bit of savings. Now I'm wishing I'd kept that bottle of scotch. Wishing I'd at least taken a double shot of it before I stalked out. Even if I don't know whether I like the stuff or not.

I should probably start door-knocking the restaurants further up the strip, before word gets around. Ha. Sometimes my thinking is so small-town. Not everyone in the city knows everyone else's business.

Brunswick Street traffic is crawling. I stand at the side of the road waiting for a gap so I can cross. Some jerk blares his horn at me as if I'm about to step in front of his SUV. I startle at the jarring blast. "WHAT'S YOUR PROBLEM?" I yell. Does he think I'm going to risk my life to put a dent in his blah-blah-custom-coloured metallic paintwork?

Why can't people be decent? Look at those drivers, smug in their cocoons of personal comfort, pushing and edging forward to own a few more inches of the road. As if getting home five minutes earlier will make all the difference to their survival of peak hour. Arseholes.

Here's a gap. I sprint across the road, then stalk up the footpath towards the music store. As I shove my hands in my back pockets, something catches on my fingernail, and I pull out a crumpled note. Harry.

4

Vacillation

My leg is jiggling under the table. Above it, I'm flicking a sugar packet back and forth. I've counted eleven tings of the bell on the café door. He's late. Twelve. This time my glance is rewarded. I swallow, mouth suddenly dry. Maybe this is a bad idea.

Harry strolls towards the café counter, hands in his pockets, surveying the room. He's just as hot as I remember, but what's with the suit again? His tie dangles loosely, à la Rat Pack style. The café's not huge. It shouldn't take him long to spot me. It's noisy though, distracting.

He's looking in the wrong section of the café. Should I wave? No. This is such a bad idea. I grab my jacket and bag and start to slide off the bench seat. If I'm quick, I can sneak off. That's if the doorbell doesn't give me away.

Too late. The grin that breaks across his face is startling, and I suddenly remember something Mum once said: "A beautiful smile doesn't make a beautiful soul." She may have been wrong. He's coming towards me. Nothing to do now but act casual.

"Going somewhere?" he asks.

A flush heats my face, and I look away because I'm crap at lying. "Just thought it might be a bit selfish to take up a whole booth with just the two of us."

He eyes my bag. "Nah. You were leaving."

"No." There's an awkward moment where we both know the truth. I sigh. "Yes." I slip back onto the bench.

"I didn't think I was that late. Sorry. I sent you a text. Didn't you get it?"

I shake my head, dig my phone out of my bag, and there's his message. "Didn't hear it. Too noisy in here." Let him think that's the reason I was about to skitter.

He slides onto the bench opposite me. "So, I bet you're wondering if the city has corrupted me? Turned me into a stalker who picks up pretty bartenders in pubs?" He lowers his voice and leans forward. "You can relax. It definitely has."

"That's a relief." I hang on the word "pretty".

He laughs. "What can I get you?"

"Nothing, I've still got my shake."

"Raspberry. Right?"

"Wow. You remember."

My sarcasm might be a little much, but he doesn't flinch. He stands. "You're not going to run away while I go order, are you?"

"Tempting, but no." I screw up my nose in lieu of adding something pithier.

It's weird, but while he's standing at the counter, I'm anticipating his return. It's as though I've been warming myself by a fire, then stepped away. Suddenly it's cold, and I'm yearning for the heat again.

"So, long time no speak," he says when he returns. "I didn't think you were going to call."

"Neither did I."

"Why did you?"

"My circumstances changed."

"Spell oblique."

I can't help but smile. "So, riddle me this. Why are you getting about in a suit when you're a student?"

"Jazz."

"What?"

"I've switched to jazz. It's goes with the scene, and I kinda like it."

"A hipster in disguise."

He frowns, looks puzzled. I stroke my chin. He does the same with his beard. "Oh. Yeah." He shrugs. "Convenient. Saves me shaving every day."

"Didn't know laziness was in fashion."

"Ouch."

That was rude. I should apologise. But I'm cranky, confused. It's not true that old friendships always pick up where they left off – even if ours feels as though it might. Too much time has eaten away at the edges of what was between us. Hasn't it?

"So, what made you call?" he asks again.

I pull out his note and smooth it over the table. The scribbled message reads:

Need a singer. Work waiting. Call me. Harry.

I turn it over. On the back is a class schedule for the Victorian College of the Arts. "I thought you might need this ... for school."

"Oh? Thanks." He folds and slips it into his pocket.

I'm relieved he's cool enough not to make a big deal of my weak excuse. Especially since I haven't figured out my own motivations yet.

"Your schedule looks busy."

"Actually ... I've decided to take a gap year." He reaches into his jacket pocket and pulls out a CD. I don't recognise the cover, but I know the artist's name: Josh Maker. He's on the radio all the time. Harry turns it over and points to the first track listed on the back – Josh's first hit single. "See that? I wrote it."

"You did not." I grab the CD and examine it closely. There, in fine print under the song title, it says: Words and music by H Carter. "Wow. I'm impressed."

Harry takes the CD back and pushes it aside. "Yes, well so were the masses for a while. Now I've got to come up with another one."

A waitress brings over an iced coffee. Harry sips it, then adds sugar. I have no idea what to say next, so I blurt the first thing that pops into my head.

"I lost my job."

"That's bad luck."

"Not really. It sucked. My boss sucked. The whole place sucked."

"No more Karaoke Queen." He smirks.

I smirk back. "At least I won't have Snap berating me for my pathetic cocktail skills. One bartending course, and he thinks he's Tom Cruise or... whoever." I can't think of any contemporary comparisons.

"He sounds like a character."

"He is. He's... my best friend."

Harry doesn't react. It wasn't a deliberate barb. It's just how things are now. Silence hangs between us. He sips. I sip. It's ridiculous, so I address the white elephant.

"Sorry I cut you off. Back then."

He looks surprised. "We're going there already?"

I shrug. "No point delaying the inevitable."

"Guess not."

"So, you're not going to dob me in?"

"For what?"

Seriously? I give him a hard look. "Let's not play games."

"I'm not a player." He says it simply. He means it. "Accidents happen."

"I'm not going back."

"No-one's making you. Although, Gran would love to know you're okay."

I shrug. "I'm sure you'll tell her." That sounded sarcastic. I'm not meaning to be ungrateful, Mary was incredibly kind to me, but I don't want reminders. "I have a new life now."

He nods. Plays with his straw. Tries to pat the blob of ice cream under the milky coffee. "Some life," he murmurs, then changes the subject before I can respond. "I'm sorry I didn't come back for Samuel's funeral."

"Yeah. Me too. Don't know if I can forgive you for that one."

I take a long pull of my shake to avoid his gaze, then look out the window. It's a bittersweet feeling. All this honesty. He reaches towards me, and I jerk away.

"Don't!" I'm shocked at myself. "Sorry, but don't touch me, okay?"

He looks awkward. "Of course. Sorry. I didn't mean to ... you have something in your hair."

I'm too embarrassed, too tense to reach up and feel what it is. This is too hard. "Well, you look great. Apart from the face wool."

His expression tells me he's having trouble keeping up. He strokes his beard. "Why? Don't you like it?"

"You look like Ned Kelly."

He shrugs. "I'll shave it off then."

"Really?"

"No."

I laugh, but then he asks how Mum is, and it's like a sandbag has landed on me.

"Okay, I suppose. I call to check how she is, but she wouldn't know who I was if I spoke to her."

"Do you miss her?"

"I guess. I try not to think about it."

He looks contemplative, as if he's deciding whether to say something. I'm pretty sure I know what it is. I change the subject.

"So, you're for real? The music, I mean. It's all happening for you?"

"Has happened. Was happening. I've got to make it work again."

"Uh huh. And what's this "work waiting" thing? What's it got to do with me?"

He smiles like I'm so amusing. "Talent. Writing one hit song does not a lifetime fortune make. I'm branching into management."

"But you're not even finished college yet."

"I'm getting ahead of the pack. I want to move now, while I've still got industry contacts from my first song. Besides, you're here now so why not? I've always liked your voice, even if you never appreciated it."

"I appreciate it. I just know my limits."

"I don't think you do. I think you're scared."

This makes me blush because he's right. "But... you want to manage me?"

"I know. Weird huh? There you were on stage after years of no contact. I thought it was a sign."

I frown. "Ridiculous."

"Maybe. At the very least, I'll land you some gigs. I've already got a few semi-regular ones myself – a couple a week – pay's not great, but together we should be able to get more. Pay the rent so to speak."

"But what would I have to do?"

He lowers his voice, making it all raspy. "Give up a pint of blood, an arm and a leg, and promise your soul to the music industry devil."

"Bloody hell."

"Exactly.

"Spell Quixote."

"Spell shut up and drink your shake."

"Fork you."

We both laugh, and it feels scarily good. I look out the window as Harry stirs his iced coffee, spoon clinking on glass. Outside, the hot north wind has picked up. It creates a little eddy of dirt with bits of discarded paper. I think how Harry left in summer, and now he's back in summer. Random. I turn to him.

"If we're going to do this, you can't tell anyone back home."

"You want me to lie?"

"It's not lying," I reason. "You're just not talking about it."

"But at least let my gran know. She's been worried sick about you."

This strikes me hard. Poor Mary. "She shouldn't be. I left a message for her, at Mum's hospice. I said I was okay."

"You've changed your mobile phone number too, so she couldn't check. That wasn't fair."

He's got me there. "Well ..."

"Just call her. Nothing bad will happen."

"I can't."

"Why not?"

"I've got my reasons. Look, I won't get all up in your business, you don't get up in mine. Okay?"

He doesn't look happy, but he nods.

5

Sanction

So here I am, outside our apartment, peering through the wrong side of the peep-hole. Snap swings the door open and gives me his "I'm disgusted" look.

"Do you know how gross an eyeball looks close up?"

"Yep. But you still fall for it every time." I grin.

He stands, hands on hips, examining me. "Trying to hide a smile, are we? Smashing, isn't he? I knew it."

"He's okay."

His smile fails. "Oh, Kitten. Tell me you didn't wear that?"

I glance down at my clothes. "What's wrong with jeans and t-shirt?"

He huffs. "Girl, does nothing I say get through to you?"

"Apparently not. Are you going to let me in, or do I need a password?"

I put a hand on his chest, kiss his cheek, then push him aside before heading straight for the kitchen and the vodka in the freezer. Snap tails me muttering something about my ponytail. I glance at the ginger kitty-themed clock on the wall with its paw-hands purrfectly and permanently stuck on five and twelve. We haven't replaced the battery because it meows on the hour, but I always like to check it's still booze o'clock.

I help myself to a shot, grimacing as it burns its way down my throat. A family-sized block of chocolate might have done the trick just as well, but I haven't done any grocery shopping this week, so there won't be anything in the fridge except maybe gourmet pate and semi-dried tomatoes – small luxuries to supplement Snap's free feeds at the pub. My free meals went out the door the moment I slapped Bob. Meh.

"Tell me everything," Snap says, leaning back against the island bench.

"Not much to tell," I say, readying to pour another shot. The first one is already limbering me up. Snap grabs the vodka from my hand before the liquid leaves the bottle.

"Not another drop until you throw me a crumb."

He carries the bottle into the lounge room. I collect a second shot glass and follow. He slides into his favourite bright-orange retro armchair and sits cross-legged, smug and elegant as always. I so love how he's blossomed into this cool self.

After we first moved in, and he got his little "bedroom business" up to a profitable standard, he started replacing our second-hand furniture piece by piece. I gave up trying to put my two cents in; the faces Snap pulled when I suggested coffee tables and sofas was enough for me to give up and let him style to his heart's content. But it's not just his taste in furniture and clothing that makes him look so amazing. If only I could rock satin the way he does. And his hair is "just so", and he's lithe, and witty, and has attitude with a capital "A". None of which I have.

We sit on opposites sides of a low glass-topped table with its little Zen garden underneath: sand, smooth pebbles, a miniature porcelain bridge, bonsai and a little wooden rake. It's exquisitely arranged. Snap spends hours organising grains of sand into perfectly behaved feng shui–inspired paths.

"So, give me the lowdown," he demands.

I shrug. "He wants to mentor me."

Snap licks his little finger and grooms a perfect eyebrow. "Is that a euphemism?"

I smirk. "He says I have something special."

Snap grabs the air in front of his chest, squeezing imaginary breasts. "You have two very special somethings, honey."

I screw up my nose.

He laughs. "I'm just kidding. I think your guy is onto something. Your voice is truly amazing. I've told you that a million times."

I wave him off. "You're exaggerating, but I love you anyway." I've never learned to take a compliment. Some people seem adept at it, as if it's an entitlement. Not me. I'd rather run and hide. But somewhere deep inside, I know he's right. I'm not stupid. A gift is a gift.

Snap takes to quizzing me like a master:

How old is he? *Twenty. I think.*

Does he have his own place? *Yes.*

Does he own it? *How the hell would I know?*

Where does he live? *In an apartment like normal people do.*

Smart arse. *Is he single? I didn't ask.*

(Apparently, I'm a fool for missing that detail)

Does he have a car? *Don't know. Didn't ask.*

(Fool again)

Does he have a job? *Doesn't need one. He wrote a hit single.*

(Impressive)

Did he buy you lunch? *Yes, even though I objected.*

Snap approves.

I'm incredulous. "How can you decide just from that? Are you sure you're not giving your blessing 'cos you think you've got a chance with him yourself?"

He looks at me as though he's indulging a puppy chewing on his fingers. "Honey, please. He's straight. Off limits for me unless you happen to toss his poor heart to the gutter. Then I'll be there to pick up the beautiful broken pieces and convince him to try another side."

Snap has no idea who's broken whose heart, but I'm not about to tell him. "Choose?"

He rolls his eyes. "Whatevs. Don't go all PC on me, Kitten. You know you'll never win."

He's right. But I don't care, I'm too busy looking at the vodka bottle, about to tell him to hand it over when I notice his I've-done-something-bad look.

"What?"

"Promise you won't be angry."

"I'm not promising anything."

"Try."

I lean forward and pick up the little rake from his Zen garden. "Tell me or the sand gets it."

"Step away from the garden."

"Tell me."

"Okay, okay. Put it down, and I'll tell you."

I do.

He takes a breath. "I called Harry."

"What?"

He grimaces. "You said you wouldn't be mad."

"No, I didn't. Snap, what did you do?"

"The night he wrote that note in the pub? I copied his number down. Just to be safe."

"Snap!"

"I worry for you. I knew he looked familiar, but I couldn't figure out why."

"What did you say to him?"

"Only that I'd break his kneecaps if he hurt you."

I'm speechless.

"Honey, don't be angry. I was just protecting you."

"Unbelievable."

"Sweetie, you're an innocent—"

"I am NOT innocent. You have no idea what I've been through."

"No, I don't. Because you're so touchy. You never open up. You have to learn to trust someone. You can't go through your whole life on self-depend mode."

"Of course I can." I go over to him and snatch the vodka bottle. "Watch me."

I return to my side of the table and sink another shot. Fuel for anger. At my own stupidity. I need to shut up before I say too much.

Snap is silent as he observes me from his chair. I'm not sure what his expression is: sad, pitying or disbelieving. I don't like any of them. He stands, and I brace myself. He'd better not be coming over to give me a hug. He pulls up his sleeve. "Remember these?"

I look at his cutting scars. Most have faded, but they're still there and always will be.

"Yes."

He unbuttons his shirt, turns his back and lets the material fall. Across his back are more criss-cross scars. Only thicker. I suck in my breath. He couldn't have done those himself.

"My father thought he could belt the homo out of me."

I stare in horror, realising only now why, even though he's developed the fittest body, taking care of it religiously at the gym, I've never seen him shirtless. It's me who moves first.

I put my arms around him. His cheek is freshly-shaven, and he smells divine as always – some foreign cologne that I can never remember the name of. He hugs me back, then pushes me away so he can button up.

"Pour us both another shot, sister. I'm cancelling my night out. It's time you and I shared some truths."

So, I tell him about Harry. I tell him more about Mum – how devastating her illness was. And how hard it was living with Samuel. But that's all. I try. I really do. But I'm afraid if the words come out, they'll swallow me, and I'll disappear somewhere dark, and I won't find my way back.

I'm traitorous for not trusting him.

6

Indoctrination

I wander over to where Harry is sitting at his baby grand. He's got a pencil between his teeth while he studies a piece of sheet music. A month into rehearsals, and I'm still tempted to press fingerprints onto the piano's lid. It's like a lake of sleek, black, reflective water you want to slip your body into. Only you'd slide off because of the angle. Too beautiful.

There's a row of three guitars suspended at an angle on the wall behind him. I recognise his old Maton from the farm. It looks rustic compared to the glossy new ones. Harry says he doesn't play them much anymore. "More opportunity playing keys. Easier for composing."

His apartment is so light and airy with its white walls and skylights, I feel grubby, especially when I've come straight from my new job at a convenience store . Polished floorboards, rugs, artwork and leather couches. He's come a long way, baby. And all this from one hit single? If this is the music industry, show me the money.

"You must be doing okay," I say. "Rent would cost a bucket load here."

Harry shakes his head. "I own it."

"Really? So why did you say you needed money to pay the rent?"

He tilts his head. "It's an expression. I've still got bills, and I can't keep living off my parents. It was enough they helped me out with this place."

"Wow, they must have done well from selling the farm." I think of the paltry sum Mum got from ours. It doesn't seem fair.

"You don't know, do you?" Harry says. "Dad invented this hydraulic sensor thing for tractors. Farmers can install and replace it themselves. Sold the patent to John Deere. Made a bundle. Now, they're off travelling again with my little sister."

"Things always seem to go right for you guys."

He looks annoyed. "We had to work for it. Like everyone else."

"Yeah, sorry." But I'm not really. Some people just seem to fall on their feet.

"And my royalties are starting to dry up, so I need to get more gigs. Either that or a real job, as they say. I gotta eat, you know?"

"Tell me about it." My new cashier gig is only part-time, but I'm beginning to wonder if all jobs suck.

He returns his pencil to between his teeth, plays a few notes, then scribbles. A crease forms between his eyebrows every time he looks up, then disappears again when he plays. Cute. Too cute. But I'm not going there. I've already made that clear.

I flop onto Harry's baby-soft couch and sip my water. He's told me to drink several glasses a day, to keep my voice hydrated. The upside is my skin feels amazing. It's never been so clear. The downside: I've never spent so much time on the loo, which doesn't help on my quieter -Eleven shifts when there's only me and I have to hold out for a chance to zip out the back. I swear I hold the record for the fastest water bottle refill and whizz-break ever.

Still, my boss doesn't miss a trick. He's obsessed with the security camera footage and always leaves reports for the staff. He's onto customer thefts, which is fine, but he also knows if we've been slacking off. "Less yacking, more stacking," he says. He calls it surveillance. I call it a dictatorship.

Not that I'm ungrateful; it's paying my share of the rent, even if my bedroom is depressing with its faded Kmart bed covers and op shop furniture. Snap's says he's going to do a makeover of my "boudoir" as soon as the cash starts rolling in from the music.

Yeah, right. I haven't seen a penny yet. "Early days," Harry says. "Another couple of months, and we'll be ready. Hit 'em hard and hit 'em good. No point going in half-baked."

Harry's busy focusing on his pencil markings – transposing, so the key hits my sweet spot. I don't pretend to understand everything. I've always learned by listening. But I know how to count bars. And I know that I sound ridiculous if I try to sing too high. I should learn theory, he says, and insists on writing down a new musical term for me twice a week. Then he quizzes me at the next rehearsal. I miss those lazy days in the hammock where I sang songs I already knew.

He puts his pencil down. "Okay, let's warm up."

He plays a scale. I baulk. Something's been plaguing me.

"Why me?"

"What?"

"Why me? You must have met stacks of other singers at college. Plenty who are way better than me. More experienced."

"Because."

"That's not an answer."

"It's the only one you're going to get." He plays my first note.

I can't let it go. "It's all too convenient. You, turning up like that."

He falls silent. Why isn't he looking at me? Then he puts on a big smile. "Luck, baby. Right place, right time."

"Well, I've given some thought to this and ..." Hell, what I'm going to say will sound ridiculous, so I just blurt it. "I think I need to use a stage name."

"Really?" He looks amused.

"Yes. It's the best way for me to stay anonymous. I know it sounds wanky but ... I've spent eighteen months hiding. Putting my real name out there is just stupid."

He waits, a strange look on his face. "Listen, I've been wanting to talk—"

I grimace as I say it. "Kitten."

"What?"

"It's what Snap calls me. What do you think?"

Harry chuckles. "If you want. It's a bit infantilising."

This gives me pause. I've never thought about it that way. I'm sure Snap doesn't mean it like that.

"But I don't think we need to worry about it at this stage," he continues, then looks at me, all serious. "Maybe it's time we talked about—"

I put my hand up. "No. I told you I'm not going there."

"Things back home aren't what—"

"No."

"Why are you being so pig-headed? It could be so much easier if you just let me—"

"I said no."

"Fine." he says, his jaw set. "Let's concentrate on getting a repertoire together." He hits my note louder. "Sing."

Peeved, I stand and vocalise the scales, sliding up and down on each vowel: a–e–i–o–u. I'm like Old MacDonald who had a farm. Only instead of pigs I've got pitch, and instead of geese I've got glissando.

It's got a hold of me now. Music. The idea of being a professional vocalist is consuming. I've been going to a few of Harry's gigs, and I can't wait to be up there with him myself. Especially after listening to the recordings he's loaded onto his old iPod for me. There's a bunch of albums by this group called Postmodern Jukebox. Their stuff is so cool. They've taken current songs and given them a 1920s flavour, swinging some and bluesing others. Listen to me, prancing around my bedroom, posing and sending air kisses to the mirror as I sing along. Hilarious.

This is the style we're aiming at. That and throwing in a few classic standards, 'cos "you gotta play to the punters". I'm down with that. It's under my skin now. Not like in Wineera, when it was just a way to spend time with Harry. It's deeper. Seeing it being made. Played for real, not just a recording.

How to describe it without going into some artsy-fartsy deep and meaningful rubbish? It's that breathlessness of watching the pre-dawn sky back home: brilliant colours wiped across the horizon, sulphur-crested cockies, hundreds of them, swarming across the reds and pinks, and the deeper blues, higher up in the sky, still pierced with stars and yet to brighten. Ha. It does it to me, music. Or maybe it's ... No. It's not Harry. But he is irritably distracting.

Tonight, he's being a pain though, drilling me over and over. It's been an hour. I've been at work at the convenience store all day, and I just want to get on with it.

"Look, I think I know when I've warmed up enough. Can we do a song now?"

"Trust me," he says. "You need this. Remember 'wax on, wax off'?"

"Wax what?"

"Mr Myagi?"

I shake my head. He may as well be talking a foreign language.

"You've never seen The Karate Kid?"

"The what kid?"

He gets up and crooks his finger at me to follow. What now? We move to the next room – a studio with a huge wide-screen television. He goes to a bookshelf crammed with DVDs and runs his fingers over the titles until he stops at one and pulls it out. "Take this. Watch it."

I roll my eyes. "I don't have a DVD player."

He sighs. "Do you have plans for the rest of the night?"

Oh, if Snap were here to hear that. "Not really..."

"Good." He points to the couch. "Sit."

I stay in the doorway and cross my arms. "Woof."

He moves to the television console and kneels to load the DVD. "I'm trying to help you here."

"Then stop treating me like a kid. Or a pet."

He twists on his knees to glance back. "Okay, I'm sorry. You're right. Will you watch this movie with me? I think it'll help you understand where I'm coming from."

"Maybe."

He fiddles with the remote control. When he's got it working, he comes over to me.

He tilts his head and looks into my eyes. "Please?"

I can't hold his gaze. I lower my eyes to his chest, his shirt, the pattern of the threads. So close. Am I imagining the warmth coming off him? I shuffle back. "Okay. But only if it comes with popcorn."

"That can be arranged."

I walk around him and sink into the couch. It's even bigger than the one in his lounge room. He hands me the remote, dims the lights and leaves me to watch the movie. Soon, there's muffled popping sounds from the kitchen. My stomach growls as the nutty smell wafts through. It seems to take forever. Eventually, I yawn and curl up in the middle of the couch. I doubt I'm going to make it to the end.

Harry appears in the doorway, a bowl in one hand, glasses and a bottle of wine in the other. Uh oh. I move over to make room for him.

"So, what do you think?" he asks.

"It's okay. Pretty dated."

"But are you getting the message?"

"Yeah. Practice, practice, practice."

"There's a little more to it than that."

He holds up a glass, questioning. I shouldn't. I'm so tired already. But what the hell? I nod.

"I ordered pizza," he says. "Pepperoni. Hope that's okay?"

"Sounds good."

We watch the screen together taking turns to dip our hands into the popcorn. Half a wine, and the dizzy warmth is spreading. I fight the urge to glance at him. Suddenly he leans in close, his breath on my ear, and it reminds me of another night. Backstage. A moment of yearning. My heart. Broken.

Harry whispers, "Just in case you were wondering, I'm not going to try anything, kiddo. Your terms. Purely business."

I cough and lean forward to put my glass down, using the motion to put a little more distance between us. "I'd like to see you try."

"Not going to happen."

"Good."

"No offence. Just so you know. Been there, done that with my previous singer."

"Oh, so I'm not the first? I knew it. What happened?"

"She got too demanding. Had to kill her."

I smirk. Is that relief or rejection I'm feeling? "Whatever. And stop calling me kiddo."

"Sorry. Force of habit."

"Try Kitten."

"Don't know if I can get used to that."

I throw a piece of popcorn at his nose. "Actually, neither do I. Doesn't sound right from anyone but Snap."

The morning after, while I'm stripping off for my shower, I catch my reflection in the mirror. I'm surprised by the smile beaming back at me. Who is that person? That can't be me. I don't do happy.

"Don't look at me like that," I tell myself. But I do anyway. It feels good.

I hop in the shower, and as I shampoo my hair, I sing a scale. Harry's told me to practise every day, twice a day when we're not rehearsing. "It helps strengthen your voice and stay in tune." (I go a little flat when I'm tired, apparently. I can't hear it, but he does). God knows what the neighbours think. I'm going off like an opera singer. Ha. Screw 'em. I've got my own Mr Miyagi. They can say "I knew her when".

Harry's not happy. I don't even have to see his face to know – it's in his body language, the way he's stalking away from me, up the hall.

"Sorry." I say it even though it's pointless.

He sits at the piano. "No point apologising if it's going to keep happening."

"It's not my fault. You know that."

"And it's not my fault I've got a gig to get to tonight, so let's make this quick."

I understand. I do. But it's freakin' irritating. I'm not choosing to be late; he's just choosing to be a dick. If I'm told I have to stay a couple of extra hours because someone hasn't turned up, I've got to do it or else it's bye-bye job.

"You need to set priorities," he says. "What happens when we start gigging together? Are you going to stroll up halfway through and shrug it off?"

I fold my arms and glower at him. "It's NOT my fault."

"I know, I know," he says. "Let's just get on with it."

I'm not ready to get on with it. This needs to stop.

"Haven't I done everything you've asked of me?"

"Yes."

"Haven't I learned every song? Haven't I practised my scales, my breathing, my stance, my delivery? Just like you said?"

"Yes."

"Well?" I raise my hands in exasperation.

"It takes one hundred and ten per cent," he says. "You're only giving it one hundred."

Is he freaking kidding me? I can't tell if he's smirking.

"Well, Mr Hollywood director, when you get me into the big time, and you're showing me the money, I'll give it two hundred per cent. For now, it is what it is. Got it?"

He smiles. "Kitten's got her claws out."

"Shut up and play." I flip my lyrics folder open to a Cole Porter classic. "Night and Day."

"You still need that?" he asks.

I'm about to throw it at him but decide to be the bigger person. Besides, I'm sure I've got all the lyrics down now ... pretty sure, anyway. I close the book and lift my chin "Happy?"

"Because ..." He leans behind the piano and pulls out a box. It's white. It's shiny. It's got an Apple logo on it and a big red ribbon.

I stare, mouth open. "For me? Purrrrr!!!"

He leans back to put it away again. "Unless you don't want it."

I reach both hands over him. "Are you crazy? Give! Give!"

He's already loaded all my lyrics onto the iPad. They're in a program called UnrealBook, and I love it. Flip, flip, a finger touch turns the pages. And it's got an alphabetical index to dig up songs in a hurry.

I hug him. "Thank you."

It warrants a huge kiss. On the cheek of course. He's looking at me as if he's the one who's been given the gift. And there's something else there in his eyes. It does my head in because I can never read what it is. It's like a chasm I can't cross. Ha. Says me who's always banging on about keeping my distance.

His touch is light on the keys as the notes lift from the piano, airy like those fluffy seedy things that carry on the wind – the ones I used to call fairies and chase across our backyard. He gives me that knockout smile, and all is right with the world. I wish I was brave enough to kiss his mouth. Spell charmed.

7

Inauguration

Am I crapping myself? Yes. This isn't karaoke in front of a bunch of drunks who don't give a monkey's. This is the Starlight Room, the casino. This is the start. How did three months go by so quickly? It wasn't long enough. Am I ready? I should be. I'm crazy excited, like a child about to take my first high dive at the local pool with every kid in my class watching. I'll never know if I can do it if I don't jump.

Harry is chill. He's worked here plenty of times. But here's me, gripping the mic stand so hard my fingers hurt. I wish I could somehow disappear behind the damned thing. I wipe sweat from my upper lip, and a nerve twitches in my right cheek. Breathe. Too sharp. I cough, reach for my glass, sip water, then scan the half dozen punters at the softly lit tables. Bless them for coming early. Better than an empty room. I wish Snap was here. Where is he? He promised.

Harry plays the first bars of my song, and my chest goes all tingly. I clack my glass on the side table. Too hard. The water spills. Crap. Now I've made a mess, and I can't remember the first line of the song.

I resort to my iPad. It's gone to sleep. I should have turned that option off. I jab at the home button. Now I have to put in the password, wait for the app to load, then find the song. Harry will be halfway through before I get there. I should have had it ready to go. Idiot.

I flash a look at Harry. He mouths, "Relax." And I think you relax. I need my lyrics, not a lesson in meditation. And why is this piano between us? Why can't I be right there, next to him, within proper hearing distance so I can tell him to wait for me?

I glance at the sparse audience again. If Snap were here, I'd have a friendly face to focus on, grinning from the front row, cheering me on. And what about the casino's entertainment manager? Is he here? He's supposed to be checking us out. Maybe it's a good thing if he's not; I'll get time to warm up.

"One note at a time," Harry calls in a loud whisper. Sotto voce. Why am I remembering useless musical terms when I can't even remember my first line?

The lyrics are up, but I don't know where Harry is up to in the song. He's told me not to worry if that happens; he'll play through to the intro a second time. Pfft. I wanted to nail it. I tap my finger on the microphone stand, keeping time. I won't miss it again. I take a breath, open my mouth and …

I'm singing. Here. In this swanky bar with a martini list so long it takes up four pages of the menu. I might be wishing I'd guzzled one or two of those martinis before I started – I would have if Harry hadn't forbidden me – but here I am, holding my own. My voice is a little husky at the bottom, strong in the middle and clear at the top. I'm doing it! I'm holding my own, and the punters don't seem to hate it.

Suddenly, I'm conscious of my shoulders up around my ears, so I force them down. Like Harry said, relax. I try to move. I'm stiff, not sexy, but I am moving. Harry says it helps ease the tension. I think I'm living proof he's mistaken. I'm like a robot attempting a hip swing. I'll get there though. Give me time.

Two songs down and Harry is blending into the start of a third. This time I don't need to turn around for reassurance. More punters drift in, and the noise level of conversation and clinking glasses increases. I don't care. I'm euphoric, feeling classy even. Only the people seated at the first few tables bother to applaud. Still, I don't care. This is my heaven.

And then it's over, and I'm so buzzy and breathless, I almost trip getting off the stage. Harry catches my arm. For a moment, I pause as a memory flickers — another stage, our school competition — and my heart twinges.

"Steady," he says.

"I did it. I did it!"

"So you did."

"Holy shit. Thought I was going to crap myself there at the start."

Harry laughs as he signals to a passing waiter, then guides me through the maze of tables. A couple of people stop us to pay a compliment. I smile, self-conscious but loving it. By the time we reach our booth, the waiter has already produced a bottle of champagne.

"Oh wow. Did you arrange this?"

"You're welcome."

We clink glasses, and I gulp nearly half of my bubbly.

"Steady. Don't write yourself off, kiddo."

Kiddo. Ugh. "We're done for tonight, aren't we? One set for the manager to check us out? I can drink as much as I want now."

"Fair call. But still—"

"Tell me. How was I? I rocked didn't I?"

He nods, mouth full of champagne.

I let go of my breath in a big sigh. "Really?"

"Really."

I grin. I could hug him. Kiss him. I gulp more champagne instead, dizzy with happiness.

"You were great." He looks at my hair. "And I know I said it already, but I really like your new style. It suits you."

I run a hand over my silky bob. It still surprises me. The restyle was Snap's idea – something to perk me up, give me confidence for tonight — even though he didn't turn up to yesterday's appointment. His hand-holding had been verbal only – a phone call because he "just couldn't get away". Whatever that meant.

"Luci is going to work miracles on you," he said.

I hung up the phone, then cried as Luci chopped the first handful, and a chunky length of long, dark hair fell to the floor. She stopped, and I had to explain that it reminded me of when Mum hacked off her own hair, that it felt as though I was losing something. I wasn't sure what. Luci cried too, but we pushed through. In the end, my reflection showed a tres cool funky cut, long at the front, shorter at the back.

I look around the casino again now. Still no Snap. Is he okay? Why would he miss tonight? He's been so excited for me. Then I remember the agent, and I turn to Harry. "Was he here? I couldn't tell. Do you think he'll give us more gigs? Do you know if he liked us? When will we find out?"

"Whoa. Slow down. Yes, he was here. I don't know if he liked us, he didn't stay the whole set. But then they rarely do. We should find out tomorrow."

"God, I hope so. It might be my only income soon."

"More trouble at work?"

"No. Yeah. I just... one minute my boss is okay with it, next he's threatening to sack me. And I can't say no to shifts on the off chance we get gigs. You know?"

Harry pats my knee. "I wish I could give you a definite answer, but you can't count your chickens in this industry. It's risky. Always was, always will be. You need to decide what you really want. And I'm not talking about working in a casino. This is just cutting your teeth. There's bigger and better out there. I think you've got what it takes."

"Really?"

"No, I just like the sound of my own—"

"Here you are!" A guy in a tailored suit approaches our booth. He's handsome in an older-guy kind of way. I've never seen someone with such immaculate hair.

Harry stands. "Tony. Good to see you."

"You too, mate." They shake hands. "I see you have your little protégé with you. Lovely. Lovely stuff."

He must be the entertainment manager. I stand and offer my hand too, bluffing confidence. "Lauren."

Tony moves to take my hand, but at the last second, snatches his hand away and pretends to run it over his beautiful hair. "Ha! Gotcha!" he says.

I laugh. What else can I do to cover my awkwardness? Now he grabs my hand and envelops it in both of his, holds firm, squeezing. "Great voice. Just lovely."

"Thank you." I try to look him in the eye, but he's glancing at my breasts, even though my neckline is high enough to be classified as nuns wear. Ugh. Again.

"Happy to have you on board," he says. "Singing a treat, up there."

"Thank you," I repeat, louder, firmer, pulling at my hand a little because he still has hold of it. He doesn't release me.

"Harry, where did you find this little gem?"

"We're long-time friends," Harry says.

"Oh. Damn. Off limits then?" He laughs, showing too many teeth and too much gum.

Seriously? What the hell?

Harry looks uncomfortable.

"Can I have my hand back, Tony?" I grin, trying to make light, when I'd really like to biff him. That'd be great, wouldn't it? Our debut night, and I take out the entertainment manager. First Bob, then Tony. It could become a habit.

He lets go, without acknowledging me. "Speak to the office," he tells Harry. "I've given my okay. They'll line you up." Then as an aside, but loud enough for me to hear, "Might want to rethink the wrapping."

As he leaves, I thump Harry's arm. "Thanks a lot."

"Ow! What was that for?"

"Little protégé? Why didn't you introduce me as your partner? I felt about this small." I make a gap between my forefinger and thumb. "We're supposed to be a team, yeah?"

"I ... yeah, of course. Don't worry about it. He's just old school."

"Didn't you see the way he was perving on me?"

"Uh, sorry. But look, we're going to have to deal with guys like that sometimes. It is what it is. If we want to sell ourselves—"

"I'm not selling myself to anybody. And what did he mean by "wrapping"? Is he talking about my dress?"

Harry flicks a look at my clothing, obviously embarrassed. He grimaces as he gently lets me have the bad news. "Your clothes are a little ... well ... underplayed. If money is the problem ..."

It stings. Snap was supposed to help me choose what to wear. I look down at my dress. In the Brunswick pre-loved clothing boutique, I thought the classic black sheath looked fabulous on me. So did the shop assistant: "It plays down your curves." I baulked at the idea of curves being something that needed playing down, but the price tag suited, so I was sold.

Admittedly, there was a whole array of glitzy dresses I could have chosen, but the evening lengths emphasised my lack of height, making me look like a dwarf in a disco ball.

For a while there, this petite, simple dress held an air of sophistication. Now it's a drab sack, and I'm doubting my shoes too. Are they not high enough? Not sparkly enough? I don't know if I can handle this roller-coaster. And I'm disappointed in my own disappointment because I thought I'd learned not to care what people think. I turn towards the stage. I'm NOT going to cry.

I watch Shelley, the headliner for tonight, testing the height of her mic stand. The crowd has thickened. She stops to wave at a familiar face, and as she moves, the fabric of her emerald dress shines and shifts over her slender figure.

"Listen," Harry is saying. "You got this. Your voice is what's doing the selling. Anything else is just smoke and mirrors. You have to trust me on that."

I sink back into my seat, disillusioned.

Harry isn't finished. "I picked it the first time I ever heard you sing. There's something unique about your voice. Something that demands attention."

We're interrupted again by a couple who stop at our booth. They're an older pair, holding hands as though they've never been apart a day in their life.

The woman speaks with a soft accent. "We just wanted to tell you how much we enjoyed your music."

Harry grins. "It's all Lauren. She's magic, isn't she?"

"You both sound wonderful," adds the man. He nods at me. "Your parents must be proud."

I nod, smile.

"Missy here has one special voice," he tells Harry. "Hang onto that one."

"I intend to," Harry says.

What is it with people thinking I'm Harry's property? Nobody owns me.

As they move on, Harry looks me in the eye. "You need more convincing?"

"They were sweet."

"They were honest. Look, work hard, ignore the crap that comes with it – that comes with every job – and in a few more weeks, they'll put us in the Ruby Room."

"What's so special about the Ruby Room?"

"It's a steppingstone. High-roller territory. Big tippers. But you've got to watch your language. Show some class. I know you're capable." He pours more champagne for us. "Once you've got more time under your belt, we'll get you some auditions for shows. I have a few connections."

"You mean stage shows?"

"Sure. It's regular work, pays well – more than the odd band gig that's for sure. You'll build a resume, get your name known. I've done a couple, playing in the orchestra. It gets repetitive, but the cast and crew make it fun. Although, I have a feeling your strength will be in recordings. Backing vocals to start with, till you find your feet. I do session work for a couple of studios now and then. Helps to have a foot in a few doors. But my point is, pay your dues here first, and you'll learn a thing or two. And creeps? They're everywhere. You'll learn to deal with them."

"Yeah, I guess the casino doesn't have a monopoly on arse-wipes."

"Spell expletive."

"Spell ... whatever."

"Come on," Harry says, "finish your drink. I'm taking you out for the best hamburger you've ever had in your life. My shout."

"Ooh, generous."

"Don't knock 'em 'til you've tried 'em."

He leads me through the warren of gaming rooms, all brightly lit with chandeliers so you can't tell what time of day or night it is, past the rows of green-felted tables with players watching their cards like birds of prey, past rattling roulette wheels and alleys of poker machines that sound like pin-ball games, each with a pinched-face hopeful sitting with one butt cheek on a stool as though they need to go to the toilet but are afraid to leave in case their machine suddenly jackpots.

Outside, the freshness of the night air revives me, and I have a thought.

"Just a mini."

I've forgotten to take my mobile off silent. I pull it out of my purse, and there it is, a text message from Snap:

Sorry, Kitten. Drinkies after?

Relief. I knew he wouldn't bail on me. It's Snap after all. And I miss him. It's ages since I've seen him properly: him coming home late from his shift while I'm asleep, then me leaving for work while he's still out of it.

I turn to Harry. "What's the name of this holier-than-thou hamburger joint?"

8

Debriefing

My stomach rumbles at the thick smell of fried onion and grilled meat. We sit in a booth next to the front window, the tabletop covered in kitsch, red and white checked plastic. Nearly every inch of wall space is covered in colourful artwork – beautiful, bold strokes merging and bursting like fireworks. "All Freda's creations," Harry tells me. They're good. Not that I know much about art, but I like them.

A slight woman in her early thirties approaches us. She has a handkerchief tied over her curly brown hair, and she's wearing an apron so over-sized I'm sure her arms wouldn't reach the bottom of its pockets. She greets us with a big smile and crooked teeth.

Harry makes to stand but she pushes him back into his seat. "Sit! Sit." She stands so close to Harry, her hip rests against his arm. She ruffles his hair.

Harry smiles as he smooths his head. "Lauren, this is my future wife, Freda."

Freda laughs. "Ah, he wishes. I offered him long ago, but the boy has big dreams." She dumps her coffee pot on the table and shakes my hand. "This one looks more likely."

I'm taken by her voice and accent. It's so sexy, it rolls around her tongue like dark honey. "I'm afraid my hamburgers wouldn't measure up. Harry's been raving about yours."

"Ah, he flatters me." She pats my hand, then releases me.

I like her immediately. She's got some sort of aura, a charisma that's disarming. She's the kind of person you can hug, even though you've just met. While she banters with Harry, I try to work out her accent. Eastern European, perhaps? Every word is pronounced purposefully, like a student who's learned a second language from a teacher who's not a native speaker.

I'm still puzzling when she plonks onto the bench, next to me, so close our elbows are touching. Obviously not shy of personal space. I shuffle towards the window, putting a few centimetres between us.

"You are not to take any trouble from this boy, okay?"

"Okay." I laugh.

"I promised to keep eyes on him for his mother. So, you come to me if there's a problem, yes?"

I'm thrown for a second and flick a look at Harry. *She knows your family?*

Harry just smiles, oblivious to my meaning.

Freda looks at Harry too. "Not much of a tongue, this one."

"Give her time," he says.

"So, Lauren. You're from Harry's town, yes? You've been friends for a long time. Was he a good boy?"

She's obviously not that connected. I push my paranoia aside. "He was mouthy. Still is." I try not to stare at her teeth, the way some of them lean and cross over, as if fighting to upstage each other.

"Mouthy?"

"Smart arse."

"Ah." She laughs. "The best kind. Let me see your hand."

"What for?"

She doesn't answer but grasps my right hand and sandwiches it between hers. Her fingers are long, her skin olive, her palms warm. Considering I'm usually contact-averse to strangers, I'm strangely calm with her touch. She closes her eyes with a frown of concentration. I glance at Harry. He pulls an I-haven't-got-a-clue face. Freda opens her eyes, peers into my palm and traces one of my creases. Here we go. I try not to laugh.

"How old are you?" she asks.

I smirk. "Aren't you supposed to tell me that?"

She ignores me. "You have been here for... nearly two years."

I nod. "Good guess."

Freda scowls at me, as though I've delivered some great insult. "It is nothing to do with guessing. Do not interrupt."

I flash another look at Harry. He must have clued her up. He shrugs as if this is normal behaviour. Freda hums as she continues her examination, then stops and tuts.

"Very unhappy childhood."

"Haven't we all?"

She looks up. "Yes," she says, softly. "Yes. Many of us."

She holds my gaze, her expression indecipherable, as though she's lost in probing my head. Suddenly, her pupils dilate so subtly I'm not sure if I imagine it. Her head moves slowly, side to side. "So sad. So much sorrow," she says. She touches my cheek and just like that I'm close to tears. She whispers, "It is not over, this thing. Forget is one thing. Forgive is another." It's a statement, not a question, and I'm hit by an overwhelming feeling that this woman totally gets me. Only it's not relieving, it's frightening.

She suddenly brightens, peers back at my palm and continues. "Hmmm, I see a stranger in your life. A musician. My, he is a handsome one, too."

I pull my hand away. "Funny. Very funny."

Freda glances at Harry, and I swear some secret message passes between them. She stands with her coffee pot. "Do not be hard on him, Lauren. He wants only the best for you. I will come back for your food orders soon."

"No hurry," Harry says. "We're waiting on a friend."

When she leaves us, I glare at Harry. "What was that?" I spit.

"Sorry." His grin looks nervous. "I should have warned you. It's a party trick she likes to do... the whole Romani gypsy thing."

"What?"

"She's from Romania, but she was sick of people joking about it, the whole cliché. So now she owns it. It's her thing."

"I don't care about her thing. You told her about me. We had a deal."

Harry frowns. "No, I didn't. All she knows is you're a friend from back home."

I stare at him, tying to discern signs of a lie. "Well ... she seemed to know a hell of a lot more than that. I feel like I've just been seen naked."

"She does that."

"So ... what? She's psychic or something?" I'm still not sure I believe he didn't rat me out.

"She's just intuitive. She knows people."

"She doesn't know me." My voice has risen, so I lower it to a hiss. "She doesn't know me. You don't know me."

Harry turns to the window, and I'm not sure if he's looking for an escape or waiting for me to stop ranting. Even if he didn't tell, he still set me up. I'm entitled to be angry, aren't I? I should leave. But I don't. It all seems ridiculous. Psychics. What a pile of crap.

We sit in silence for a while, both staring out the window. And now I'm wondering how much Freda does actually know about me. It's not as if she stuck a flash drive in my ear and downloaded my history, but it sure felt like she accessed something. Something nobody else needs to know. Something that's... not over. I can't think about that.

A crusty looking woman pushing a supermarket trolley crammed with odds and ends is shuffling past. As she nears our window, she comes up close and peers in. Her skin is creviced with age and weathering, the fibres of her woollen hat, pulled low over her ears, are unravelling. We're almost face to face when she pokes out her tongue, then grins. I'm so shocked I pull away from the window. Harry laughs and so do I, even though I'm not finished with being angry.

"You okay?" Harry asks.

"Yeah. What I really feel like doing is curling up into a ball. I'm tired as hell. It's been a long week."

And it has: final rehearsals, hefty shifts at the convenience store, then today rushing home to shower, getting myself ready for tonight, warming up my voice, stressing because I couldn't get my freakin' hair the same way the hairdresser had it, then tramming it from Fitzroy to the casino. My stage nerves were a whole other world of pain.

"Does it get any easier?" I ask.

He's puzzled.

"The stage. The nerves."

"Soon you'll own that stage."

His voice is willing me to agree with him, but I can't meet his eyes, so I find myself eyeing his dark-blond beard. I still don't like it, all that hair, but damn him for being so hot.

"Forgiven?" he asks.

"Spell never."

"Harsh."

I shake my head. "I don't know if I can do this."

"Do what?"

"This." I splay my hands as if encompassing the world around me. "The whole thing. All of it. Don't get me wrong, I loved being up there, with you, but I forgot how scary it is. People watching you. I nearly crapped myself tonight. And other stuff keeps going round and round in my head. I mean, what if we don't get enough gigs? My boss is on my back about working weekends, I can't commit to gigs if I have to work, I can't pay my rent if I don't work. And ... and ..."

Damn it. I cover my face, embarrassed, tearful. Harry tries to take my hands. I pull away. "Don't."

"Hey." he says softly, handing me a handkerchief.

Who carries hankies these days? But it's soft and clean and nice. I sniff and wipe my nose. I keep my head lowered, hoping my fringe is covering my eyes. I can't let him see me. I'm such a wuss. I should get up and walk out. But I'm exhausted. I want someone else to take the burden. Make the hard decisions for me. Something that couple in the casino said, about my parents being proud. It hit home. I suddenly really, really miss my mum.

"Lauren, look at me. Hey, I know it all seems overwhelming right now. But it will get better. I promise. You've been working so hard for this. Don't let it go now."

"And then you go and... and... psyche me with Freda."

"Yeah, maybe that was the final straw. Sorry, but I did it for a good reason."

I look at him. I'm sure there's mascara streaked down my face, but I don't care.

Harry's forehead creases, and he puts on a ridiculous face. "Ah, yes vell... you veel 'ave to trust dis very 'andsome musician and know dat dis very 'andsome musician 'as your int-er-est at 'eart."

He almost pulls a smile from me. Almost. "That's terrible. Nothing like her."

He points to my nose. "You've got a little something..."

I blow my nose again, refusing to let him distract me. "Okay, so let's hear your reason. This better be good. I'm too tired for bullshit. I'm too tired for..." My stupid tears start all over.

He rubs my hand. "I'm all out of hankies, sorry."

"God. I don't know what's wrong with me." I take deep breaths, trying to calm. Is it PMT? When am I due next? "This is so—"

"Helloooo! Oh, Kitten. Are you crying because I missed your debut?"

Holy crap! I immediately drop my pity-fest. Snap has a huge stitched gash above his left eye and purple and yellow bruising over his cheek and jaw.

"Snap!" I stand to cup his face. But he tilts his head back.

"No touching the merchandise." He sniffs. "Still hurts."

I settle for a gentle hug instead, but even that makes him cringe. I pat the bench next to me. "What happened?"

He sits and makes an elaborate show of adjusting my messed-up fringe. "Love your hair, Kitten. Luci did an amazing job. I knew she would. Are you okay? Big night?" He takes a napkin and tries to clean beneath my eyes, like a mother would a dirty-faced child. I'm lucky he didn't lick the tissue first. I bat him away.

"Don't worry about me. What happened to you?"

"I'm sorry I missed you. I really wanted to come, but I didn't want this," he says, framing his face with his hands, "to upset your big night. How did it go?"

"Good. But, Snap, your poor face." I refrain from touching him, although my fingers are itching to stroke his bruising.

He tosses his head. "Oh, just a little altercation out the back of the pub. You're not the only one who can hold their own." He turns to Harry and smiles, all coy.

Harry looks baffled, concerned and surprised, all at once. "Someone attacked you? Why?"

"Story for another day."

"No, it's a story for now," I say. "You can't turn up all black and blue and brush it off. Tell me."

Snap huffs. "You won't like it."

"I already don't like it."

He presses my hands onto the table, holds them there as if he expects them to fly up and do something crazy. "Okay. Just remember I was only defending you."

I bite down my panic and let him speak.

"So Bob is going on and on about how the new bar girl is too slow, too stupid, too chatty with the customers – she's not, she's an absolute sweet thing – but whatever..." Snap forgets to hold my hands because he's too busy with his own gestures of disgust. "And he starts on about how the last bitch left him in the lurch. It was too much, so I told him to shut his pie hole. Next thing he starts calling me a faggot and all sorts. God, I thought I was back in my dad's house. Then he smashes me one. Punches me right in the head."

"Snap!"

"Don't worry, honey. I'm a bit bruised and battered is all. I gave him just as good back, for both of us." He flexes his bruised hand. "That fucker's going to need a good dentist." Snap looks proud. "Not very lady-like, huh?"

Harry looks incredulous. "This is the bar manager, yeah?"

I nod and ask warily, "Did you call the police?"

Snap pats my knee. "It's okay, honey. I left your name out of it."

"Snap. I didn't mean—"

Snap looks at Harry, then me. "What? He's gonna know about it, eventually."

Harry looks puzzled. "Know what?"

Oh hell, this is not good. It's none of Harry's business. It's nobody's business. I just want the whole shitty thing to go away. "Nothing—"

"He sexually harassed her," Snap cut in.

"What? When was this?"

I hold up my hand. "It doesn't matter. I dealt with it. It's not your business."

"Of course it's my business. I'm your manager. Anything that happens, I need to know about."

I'm sure my expression is conveying my incredulity. One gig together, where nobody gave a toss, does not make me some high-profile star who needs spin doctoring. And not only that, is he actually more worried about what people will think than the fact I was molested? I speak in a monotone, hoping it gives me a sense of authority.

"My private life is mine."

Harry doesn't back down. "Not if you're serious. Once you hit the big time, everything you've said and done in the past is fodder for the press."

I almost choke. "Big time?" He's taking this all too seriously. "We're working in a freakin' casino lounge."

Snap raises a finger. "Shhh, kiddies. Let's save this for another time."

I glare at him. "You started it."

"Yes, well, now I'm finishing it. Tonight should be a celebration. Come on, play nice. Let's start again." He holds out his hand to Harry. "Lovely to see you again."

Harry looks unsure of what to do with Snap's bruised hand. He settles for a loose, up and down motion of Snap's fingers. I make one of those childish harrumphing noises. "I forgot you two already know each other."

Harry and Snap both look at me. Snap does his one-eyebrow-lift thing. "Something else up your girdle?"

"Nothing. I just don't like people poking into my private things." It only takes a second before I realise the double entendre. Snap opens his mouth, and this time I raise a finger. "Don't even." Now it's his turn to harrumph. Heh. So, that's where I get it from. I take the biggest breath and let it all out in one huge sigh. This night has lasted a century. I need sustenance. "Hamburgers, anyone?"

While we wait, we make small talk, commenting on the eclectic nightlife on Acland Street: the tourists in their crisp white runners, the regulars in shredded jeans and t-shirts, teens with wild hair, chunky boots and skirts so short you can tell what colour undies they're wearing. I wish I had their confidence.

Finally, the burgers arrive. Harry is right: they are the best ever. There's hardly any conversation while we tuck into the hot succulent meat, juice running down our faces and bits of salad squeezing between our fingers. We make feral noises and laugh. It's all disgustingly good.

I'm nearly finished my burger when Harry says, "So I have some news."

I stop chewing. What now? I can't deal with anything else tonight. I hope whatever it is doesn't need my brain cells to make a decision. Those babies are in a food coma.

"Do you have a passport?" he asks.

I shake my head.

"Huh. Well, we'll have to get you one in a hurry. We're going on a cruise."

I almost choke on my last tasty bite. "What?"

"How does six weeks in the South Pacific sound?"

He's got my attention. I make big eyes at him and reach for my milkshake to clear my throat.

"I've been offered a gig on the Emerald Princess. It's an emergency fill-in position for a duo who couldn't complete their contract. Leaves in a couple of weeks. You don't get seasick, do you?"

"I don't know."

"There's just one catch: we'll have to share a cabin."

I sense Snap instantly perk up. He nudges me under the table, but to his credit he remains quiet.

Harry holds up his hands. "No strings. No funny biz. Just work. It's not as glamorous as it sounds. The cabins are usually in the belly of the ship, no air, no light, late nights, and you get woken up early by the anchor clanging. But the pay is good, and I think the experience of solid daily gigs will be invaluable for you."

"But ... what about the casino gigs?" I ask. This is all moving so fast.

"They can wait. Plenty of musos on their roster."

"But ... do they know I've only done one gig?"

"They don't need to know that. They trust me. And I trust you. Have some faith in yourself."

"You've done cruise work before?" Snap asks.

"Yeah, a couple of times during semester breaks."

I'm mute with panic.

Snap chuckles and rubs my back. "She's tired. She needs time to think. Let's sleep on it, shall we?"

I nod. Good plan.

I catch Snap's wink at Harry. Then his grimace from the pain.

9

Cataclysm

Sleep. Oh god. Sleep.

"Rise and shine, Kitten. It's nearly eleven. Upsies."

Snap opens the blinds, and I think I know where the term blinding comes from. I'm like a kid not wanting to get up for school, all moans and doona over my head.

"You suck."

"Don't blame me, honey. It's all self-inflicted. "Vodka is my best friend" and "I never get a hangover". Sound familiar?"

I peek my nose out. "Did I say that? I think my BFF in a bottle just dumped me, big time." Snap puts a cup of something on my bedside table. It doesn't smell like coffee. "I hope that's not some weird herbal brew," I grumble. "I need caffeine. And Panadol." I pull the doona back over my head. Snap tries to yank it back down but I'm holding tight.

"Such a child."

"Coffeeeeeeeeeee!"

"Alright. Anything to stop that shrieking. And you call yourself a singer."

I wait until I'm sure he's gone because I've realised I'm naked except for my undies. Did I do that? Or him? Oh hell, what's the difference? He's my sista from another missus. Ooh, bad. Note to self: strike rapping career off bucket list.

He's draped my bunny-patterned dressing gown over the end of my bed. I pad out to the lounge room, where he's sucking on a grapefruit segment. Bleh. At least he's made some buttered toast for me.

"Ta." I give him a kiss on his good cheek. He looks fresh. How does he do that? His night was just as late as mine.

"Pleasure, treasure. Sit, sit. Dig in."

I collapse into an armchair, taking the toast with me and shoving half a piece in my mouth. I can't chew fast enough to get it into my needy stomach.

"Coffee's brewing," he assures me, still sucking on his grapefruit.

I'm looking at his bruises. The morning light isn't doing them any favours. "Are you okay?"

"Mmm. A little tender."

"So, fill me in on what's happening with Bob."

His face scrunches, and I'm not sure if it's the grapefruit or the mention of Bob.

"Nothing"

"What?"

"What am I going to do? Go to the police? How's that going to work out for us?"

The P word. I drop the rest of my toast back on my plate. He's right. So far, we've been lucky. Who knows if they have some sort of digital record on us that'll ping if we come up on their radar.

"What about your job?"

"I'll get something else. I know enough people."

Snap suddenly sounds resigned, and I realise the freshness about him is artificial – all hot shower, moisturiser and hair product. His shoulders are sagging, and he has a slight double chin, which he usually hides by holding his head forward.

"What's wrong?" I ask.

"I should have quit when you did. I guess I thought someone needed to protect the other young things still working there."

An awful heaviness hits my stomach, and I don't think it's my hangover. If we were normal people, we could both report Bob. But we're not. When are we ever going to stop worrying about the past?

"Snap, maybe it's time I—"

"Don't even think about it."

He understands my fears, and it's a relief. I'm such a coward.

"Stop worrying, honey. Eat the rest of your toast, it's getting cold. I'll get your coffee."

"I'll get it," I offer. Then I just sit there because I'm too lethargic to move.

Snap gets up. "I need to top up my tea anyway."

He moves to the kitchen leaving me to ponder. What if neither of us did anything? What would happen? Nothing. Bob would still be an arsehole, and we would just get on with our lives. I've still got my convenience store job, and the cruise work ... the cruise work! Oh wow. I grab my toast again. My appetite is back.

Snap comes back with two cups. "We've run out of milk. Black okay?"

"Anything is okay as long as it's got caffeine in it."

He passes me a cup and holds out a couple of Panadol. I smile, grateful. "Thanks, Mum."

While he sits and dunks his herbal tea bag, I gulp the tablets with a burning sip of coffee, then I close my eyes and bury my nose in my cup, snorting up the aroma, waiting for the tablets to kick in. If it wasn't for the feeling of being stared at, I could fall asleep in my cup. It's almost painful to open my eyes again.

"What?"

"Tell me what you've decided about the cruise. I think you're crazy if you don't do it. I would."

"Of course you would. You think he's hot."

"Don't you?"

I shrug. "He's okay."

Snap puckers his lips. "Don't play coy. Nobody does it better than me. Here ..." He gets up and goes over to his laptop at the kitchen bench. "I've been looking it up online. The Emerald Princess. It looks divine. It's huge."

I drag myself up and look over his shoulder. It does look amazing, all glossy white and ... cruisey. "Let's see the rooms."

He clicks a tab and a picture appears of a spacious suite with a large bed and porthole.

"Yeah, but that's not the type of room we'll have. It'll be crew quarters, all cramped."

"All the better to get you laid, my sweet. Gotta break the seal at some stage. You don't want cobwebs where the sun don't shine."

A curl of alarm unfurls in my chest. I slap his arm to cover my uneasiness. "Shut up. It's business. He's managing me."

Snap gives me a sideways look. "That's one way to put it."

"We're just friends."

"Crapolla. I see the way he looks at you. Don't refuse a gift horse. Especially, one that's well—"

"Stop! Anyway, if he's so uptight about knowing everything about me as my manager, what about my burning down Samuel's house? He must know about it already. Mary would have told him. Why hasn't he mentioned it?"

"I don't know. Why haven't you asked him?"

I shrug. "Too hard basket."

Snap strokes my hair. "Maybe it's no big deal. Technically, it was your house to burn."

"Maybe is too big a risk. And what about my store job? My boss will never give me leave for the cruise. He'll sack me."

I go back to my comfy chair and flop. Snap follows suit and picks up his tea. "Big deal. It's a crap job anyway. Do the cruise. You know you want to. The boy is hot."

I roll my eyes. He's right. Six weeks in the South Pacific is an enticing prospect. But then there's the whole sharing a room thing. I'm sure Snap's motive is my happiness, but he'll also want a vicarious report of all the gory details in a daily blog: Sordid and Sexy at Sea.

"One sweet day you're going to say, "Snap, you were sooo right. Will you be my best man?" And I will say, "No, honey, but I'll be your bridesmaid"."

"Funny. When I was buying my little black dress yesterday, I saw the pinkest, frilliest, frou frou gown. You'd look gorgeous in it."

"Honey, I am not your average camp. I am dramatic."

I'm grinning into my coffee, and when I look up there's a strange expression on Snap's face. He's gone pale, and there's a twitch in his left eye – the one with the stitches above it. Then it all happens at once: his face goes slack, his bottom lip droops, and his hand falls limp, dropping his tea into his lap.

"Snap!"

I'm out of my chair and by his side as his head falls forward, chin resting on his chest. He's making a strange "nnnnnnn" sound. I kneel and try to lift his head. It's all wobbly and heavy. "Snap! Snap! Speak to me." I'm worried about the hot tea all over his legs, but I'm more panicked about what's going on in his brain; his left eye is all pupil – huge and black. I gently pat his face. "Snap? Can you hear me?" I pull his damp robe away from his lap and fan his legs. They're splotched bright red.

You hear about this sort of thing – signs to look for and stuff — but those stories never seem real. It's something that happens to other people – someone who knows someone who knows someone. This is real. I think he's seriously having a stroke.

I brush his hair from his face and plead with him. "Snap? Snap? Can you hear me? I'm calling an ambulance." He's still making the weird noise, and once I let go of him, his body flops over the arm of the chair. I lean him back again, then look for my phone, his phone, any phone.

The operator asks questions, so many questions. I need to get him on the floor if I can, for his own safety.

"Okay, Snap. You're, okay. I'm just going to move you." I push his beloved feng shui table out of the way, and the sand skitters. "Sorry. You can fix it later." I think I'm talking more to reassure myself than him. Standing beside his chair, I lean him forward a little and dig my hands under his armpits from behind. "Here we go." God, he's heavy for someone so svelte. I edge him down, bit by bit, until he slips onto the floor in a big lump, then straighten him out onto his side with a cushion under his head.

"Now what?" I ask the operator.

"Check his breathing again."

"Yes."

"Good."

"Make sure the door is unlocked."

I do.

"Stay with him until the ambulance arrives." Stay with him? Where the hell does she think I'd run off to?

I settle by his side to wait, then remember the hot tea. It's probably too late to stop a burn. Should I get a wet towel anyway? Is it okay to leave him for a minute? I run to the bathroom. When I get back, his eyes have closed, and he's stopped making that noise. I check his breathing again. Still there. I lay the towel over his legs. Now there's nothing I can do but hold his hand until the ambulance arrives.

It's 1.15 am when my phone vibrates. Somehow, I've managed to fall asleep under the glaring waiting room lights. It's a message from Harry. Outside. Take your time. He's in the car park. He can't leave his car because he's come straight from a gig, and his gear is piled in the back. He's been amazing. Going back and forth from the hospital to get me a change of clothes, staying with me until he needed to leave for his gig, and now he's back to collect me.

I rub my hands over my face, yawning as I walk over to the nurses station. The duty nurse has changed. This one's a stout fifty-something with glasses on a chain around her neck. She's on the phone. I lean on the counter and wait. More waiting.

"Yes?"

Her voice jolts me. I must be in La La Land.

"Um, I wanted to check on... George. George Theodakis."

She taps on her keyboard and examines her screen. "Still in ICU. No change. Sorry, I can't tell you any more than that."

I drop my head on the counter, trying not to let my frustration take over. She's just doing her job, but they've been giving me the same story since Snap came out of surgery this afternoon. "Please. Can't I see him for just a second?

I've been here all day. All night. Has he woken up yet? Is he conscious?"

The nurse looks as if she's going to give me the official are-you-a-relative line – which I've already had from the previous nurses who I should have lied to – but she weakens and reads her screen again. "It doesn't say much else. Honestly. This kind of operation is complex. He may not wake up for hours or even days. Go home. Get some sleep." Blah blah blah. "Check back in the morning." Blah blah blah.

"It is morning," I snap.

She ignores me.

Okay, I get it. I'm a dick. "Thanks." Sincerity escapes me.

Harry is leaning against his car, arms folded. He looks beautiful – tall and lean in his black suit and white shirt, open at the neck. Goddamn sexy. I can't believe these thoughts are in my head while Snap is in there fighting for his life. I must be delirious. It's my exhaustion talking.

"Okay?" he asks.

I shake my head. I don't speak because I know I'll start crying if I do. Then he makes it worse. He gives me a big hug, and it's like he's squeezing my tears out. The first sob hurts like hell. I've been holding it down so hard, it's as if it's ripped my throat on its way out. We stand like that for ages, him hugging, me shaking and bawling like a kid, until I'm drained.

He releases me, digging in his pocket for a handkerchief. Bless him and his hankies. He opens the car door, and I sit, all snotty, teary and nose-blowing.

"Home?" he asks.

I don't want to go back to an empty apartment. Not yet. "Can we get some fresh air?"

We head to St Kilda beach. It's a warm night, and the breeze is soothing as we walk along the esplanade. Harry tucks my arm through his. It's comforting. Cosy. Like he's taking the burden for a while. We must look like a romantic couple. On a different night we might be.

"Any change?" he asks.

I shake my head. "I don't think so. Either that or they won't tell me. I'm not a relative."

"Does he have any relatives here?"

"His dad's back in Wineera. Snap would kill me if I called him. His grandmother lives here, but they don't speak. I found her number in his phone. I don't know if I've done the right thing, but I left her a message. I hope he doesn't hate me for it when he wakes up."

We approach a pier and turn onto it in unspoken agreement. I lose myself, listening to the hiss and drag of waves in the murkiness a metre or two beneath our feet. Across the bay, the lights from Port Melbourne warp and flicker in the humid air. The West Gate Bridge looks like an arc of fairy lights.

"Can we talk?" he asks.

God, there goes my pulse. Thump. Thump. Thump. I don't think I have any energy left in me, but my heart thinks otherwise. "Okay." There's a bench up ahead, and I point to it. "Let's sit." I don't think I can cope with walking and talking.

The bench is covered in bird poo. Harry starts to take off his suit jacket.

"Are you kidding?" It'll ruin it." I shrug out of my cardigan. "It's old," I assure him.

He tries to refuse.

"Don't be a masochist, or macho, or whatever it is. Just sit."

"You're falling down with your vocabulary," he says.

"And who's to blame for that?"

The cardigan doesn't stretch far so we sit close. I'm half expecting him to put his arm around me, or at least rest it along the back of the bench. He doesn't. It's disappointing. I was enjoying our earlier cosiness.

"I've been thinking," he says.

"Hmmm?"

"About the cruise job. I know this is a really crappy time for you."

Oh shit. He's changed his mind.

"Maybe it's a bad idea."

There. He's slammed the door before I've had a chance to put a foot through it. I want to shift away from him, but there's the bird poo. He leans forward, massages his palm with his thumb.

"I'm thinking maybe I've put too much pressure on you, too soon."

I feel sick. As if the ground has heaved beneath me. My voice becomes tiny, like a child too afraid to ask if a parent still loves them after they've been bad. "Are you calling it quits on me?"

"No, no. It's just the timing is bad. And to be honest, I don't think you really know what you want at the moment. Maybe we should ease off for a while."

He couldn't be more wrong. I do know what I want. I want all this confusion to go away. I want Snap to wake up and be alright, and for everything with Bob to have never happened. I want to keep making music, just without – like he says – the pressure.

"Look, take a couple of days to decide. Be with Snap. Have a think about your priorities. If you don't want to go ahead with the music, well... you're smart ... you'll figure it out."

"Can't be too smart if I stuff up my career after one gig."

He's looking at me, not saying anything. God, I hate that. He's supposed to be contradicting me. Telling me everything's going to be alright. That I shouldn't worry. That he believes in me.

I hasten to the fill the silence. "You know what? When I was sitting in the waiting room today – and I know this sounds stupid, because I know I'll never be a huge celebrity – there were all these trash mags with exclusives on Hollywood stars. You know, who's sexing who, who's wearing what, who said this, did that, and I thought... I couldn't live like that. Couldn't have people in my face all the time."

He laughs, and I feel like an idiot. Tiny.

"Well," he says, "every superstar started off as a kid with a dream. Why shouldn't that be you?"

"For a start, I'm not a kid."

"I didn't mean ... You just have to believe."

"Like in fairies?" My laugh sounds forced.

"And those people in those magazines?" he says. "They're not real talents. They're sensation seekers, ready to do anything for publicity. You don't need to do that if you're solid in what you do. Your work speaks for itself."

"Yeah, but I'm not solid."

He looks at me then, his eyes intense. I think he's going to say something I don't want to hear. The truth. That he's wrong about me. I want to look away but can't.

"You will be. Trust me. More solid than any over-produced, throw-away, one-hit-wonder wannabe."

Oh, god. It's only now I realise how much I care about what he thinks. "Stop. You're embarrassing me."

He grabs my hand and gives me one of his killer smiles. I melt. If this were a movie, I'd throw my arms around his neck and lose myself in his... his ... I don't know what. But I would. He's still silently watching me, and I'm sitting here trying not to imagine his kiss on my mouth and his hands on my body.

The spell is broken when he returns my hand to my lap. "Come on," he says. "I'll drive you home before we do something stupid."

As he makes to stand, I grab his arm. He sits again, waiting for me to speak, but I can't get my words out. I'm staring dumbly thinking: Do something stupid. Do it.

"What is it?" he asks.

"Do you know what you really want?"

He studies my eyes. If he can't read what's going on in them, he must be blind. I'm waiting, both hopeful and afraid that I might or might not end up getting what I'm pushing for.

"We can't always have what we want," he says.

"Hang on, that's not what you just said. You said, "if you believe". Why doesn't that apply to you?"

"Because I'm choosing to be your manager right now."

"And if I don't want to be managed?"

He hesitates. Why won't he admit his feelings?

He stands, hands in pockets. "Come on. Let's not ruin it."

You just did.

We head back to the car, without my arm through his. Did we just lose something that was almost real? A piece of my heart is back there on the bench and every step we take, it's further away. Soon there'll be no hope of retrieving it.

We drive in silence until we pull up outside my apartment. He clears his throat and fiddles with the car keys, stalling. I'm half hoping he'll insist on walking me to the door. Maybe even stay. I'm on the verge of asking if he'd like a coffee, when he shoots me down.

"I'm going to make it easy for you," he says. "I'll find someone else to do the cruise gig with. It's not fair on you to deal with all this pressure. When I get back, we can figure things out."

Click. He's turned the lock in that slammed door, and he's walking away with the key. I pretend to study the silver studs on my shoulder bag, pressing my thumb into each one, working my way around the strap. Images of white sand, palm trees and warm water I'll never feel, slipping away. I'm gutted.

"You know what?" I say, "I just realised I still don't have a passport."

"Well, that's that then. I'll get a mate to fill in with you at the casino, so you don't lose any gigs while I'm away. It'll be a good experience for you – working with someone besides me."

"Okay. Sounds good." It doesn't.

"So, we're okay?" he asks.

"Yeah."

"Sure?"

"Yeah, sure. You do what you gotta do. I'll be fine. I'm going to take my tired butt upstairs. Night." I brave a quick peck on his cheek. "Thanks for today."

"Night," he says. There's doubt in his voice.

As I step outside the car, the air is much cooler. For a second, I think about pulling on my cardigan. But wrapping myself in bird poo wool isn't appealing. I hurry to the footpath. Harry winds down his window and yells.

"Call me if you need anything. With Snap, I mean."

I wave.

The apartment feels cold and shrunken, without Snap. Like a loaf of bread that's been left in the freezer too long. The kettle lid is broken and rattles as the steam begins to rise. Snap's been meaning to buy a new one for ages. I should have got off my lazy butt and done it myself. How much do I rely on him?

I lie on my bed and sip hot chocolate in the fuzzy light of my portable telly, hoping my body will hurry up and realise it's time to sleep. Now that it can, it won't, and all I'm thinking about is how to recapture a moment that never happened: the feel of Harry's lips on mine, the warmth of his breath, the taste of him.

My phone vibrates on my bedside table. I've forgotten to turn the sound back on after the hospital. It's Harry.

"Okay?" he asks.

I nod, then realise I need to answer. "Mmmm."

"I'm worried we're not on the same page," he says.

"No?"

"I'm not dumping you... from the music. I'm not giving up on you. You know that don't you?"

"Yeah. Well, no... I wasn't sure."

"You're not dumped."

I close my eyes. Here's the fatigue I've been waiting for. My hand trembles so much I can hardly keep the phone pressed to my ear.

"Still there?" he asks.

"Just."

"Okay. I wanted to make sure you're alright and ... I thought ... if you want to stay at my apartment while I'm away, to be closer to Snap at the hospital, you can."

"That's really nice of you."

"Sleep on it," he says.

"K."

"Hey?"
"Yeah?"
"Flip side."
"What?"
"You don't remember."
I pause. "Yes, I do." And I smile because we still have our song.

It's been over a week. The linoleum floor muffles my steps, and murmurs from televisions and visitors' voices drift into the hallway. As I pass one room, the stink of disinfectant and faeces hits me. I gag. Imagine being so old or sick you can't even make it to the toilet. Awful. Humiliating. It makes me wonder if Mum is at that stage now. I can't think about that.

Here it is: room 30B. It's right opposite a nurses station – so they can keep an eye on him, I suppose. I pause and give a querying look to the duty nurse as I point to Snap's room.

She nods and smiles, seems to recognise me. "He's still comatose, but you can talk to him."

The curtains are partially drawn across the window. They do that in the mornings, so the sunlight doesn't hit his face. The bed next to his is empty, and I briefly wonder if the old man who occupied it the past few days made it home to his family or ... not. I step forward quietly and move to Snap's side. God, he looks like death: his skull is all bandages; his face gaunt, pale as the sheets he's lying on. There's a breathing tube taped to his mouth. I thought I could handle this, but I can't. I'm scared as hell.

I sit, the vinyl chair creaking, and I worry the noise might wake him. That's a stupid thought. I want him to wake up. "Snap?" I pick up his hand. It's cold and dry. What do

I say? "How are you?" seems ridiculous. I should tell him everything's going to be okay. The nurses say that words do get through, even if a comatose patient can't answer, somewhere deep inside, they hear you.

I don't know if everything will be okay, though. I wish he'd wake up and smack me for worrying. "Get a grip, girl," he'd say. "I'm not dying." And I'd say, "You freakin' better not be."

It's weird. He doesn't look unconscious. He looks as though he's sleeping. Then again, what does unconscious look like? What's the difference? Are we unconscious when we sleep?

"Hey," I whisper. "I found your phone, so I called a couple of your friends. They said they would visit. And ... don't be angry, but I called your gran. I know, I know, you said she doesn't care but, well, her number was still in your phone, so I figured you haven't written her off. And, you know, sometimes people change and ... she's family. Someone should know what's happened to you. I mean ... if you don't pull through... someone needs to ..." I take a breath. This is not going in the direction I planned. Positive. Be positive.

"So, here's a bonus: I didn't call your dad. I figured, wheelchair or not, he'd be able to whoop your butt with you out cold, so ... no dad. But anyway, your gran didn't answer. I'll keep trying. If she fobs me off, well, too bad. But she's family, you know? She has to care."

I sit and wait. And wait. The shadows in the room move slowly as the sun arcs into afternoon. The soft thud and hiss of Snap's ventilator mesmerises me, while the padding and squeaking of nurses' rubber-soled shoes, the beeping of call buttons and drift of passing conversations all fade into the background.

At some stage, a tight, heavy thing builds inside me. I think it's fury. Yes, it is. I'm so freakin' angry because this didn't need to happen. I didn't ask Snap to interfere. I'd already walked away from the pub. Forgotten about it. Why should I have to deal with the Bobs and Samuels of the world? I don't have that sort of power. I wish I did, but I don't. And now look – for eight days my precious friend's been in some space I can't reach, and he may never, ever wake up.

10

Circumspect

The sparkly dress hangs as if it's been tailored for the ridiculously tall and impossibly thin mannequin on the pedestal.

"It'll look amazing on you," the salesgirl says. She's been following me around, suggesting bits of clothing that maybe a fifteen-year-old would wear.

"Amazing isn't my thing," I tell her.

Besides, I suspect she would say a baggy t-shirt that's been rolling about on my bedroom floor for a week would look amazing on me – if it made her a dollar.

"It's vintage," she says.

"What? Second-hand?" How can something used cost a hundred and eighty freakin' dollars?

"Vintage design," she says unblinking.

She's good. She has this way of communicating her superiority without being obvious. There must be some special school that slinky, blonde-tressed salesgirls attend to learn this Zen kind of put-down. Who knew? Snap would. I wish he were here with me. Why won't he wake up? I can't do this fast lane without him.

I sigh. "Okay, what the hell. Nothing else seems as if it'll fit."

"Great." She looks me up and down in a glance. "Size twelve."

Her tone doesn't leave room for argument. I eye her sideways. How does she do that?

She flips through the rack and whips out a dress. "I'll put it in the fitting boutique, shall I?"

She pronounces "boutique" with an emphasis on the "que", like "boutiquay". Maybe not "quay", more like "kah", "boutikah". What is that, anyway? Code for tiny, little upright coffin with surround mirrors that make you look taller and slimmer than you really are, until you try the dress on again in your bedroom and go WTF?!!! Did I grow a spare tyre on my way home?

"Special occasion?" the salesgirl asks.

"Mmm." I can't be bothered explaining.

"Oh, where are you going?"

Damn her. I explain: I'm a singer, blah blah blah, and we've got our first gig in the casino's Ruby Room tonight. I don't tell her I'm super excited because the casino's entertainment manager has promoted us so quickly, or that I'm sad too because it's my last gig with Harry before he leaves for the South Pacific.

The salesgirl is buzzed and promises to bring her friends along to see me, obviously unaware it's a restricted room, and she and her dinky little friends will have fat chance of gaining entry. Weird, now it should be my turn to feel superior. But I don't. Instead, I smile and try to sound sufficiently grateful for her help so that she'll leave me alone with the dress.

It's a little tricky to get on, and the sequins scratch my arms when I zip up. I look in the mirror and OMG. She's right.

The dress looks freakin' amazing. Just enough cleavage, just enough of a split in the side, and the perfect red for the Ruby Room.

It's crazy busy here. Apparently, weeknights at the casino are no different from weekends. I guess school nights are irrelevant to high rollers. The décor is a cut above the Starlight Lounge: all crystal chandeliers, lush red carpets and velvety chairs, but that's as far as the ruby theme applies.

Harry waves when he sees me. I dump my gig bag on the stage and take my jacket off. He whistles, then grins.

I look all innocent eyes at him. "What?" I know exactly what, but I want to hear it anyway.

"You look stunning."

"Thanks." I don't even blush.

We kick off with a few standards and Harry is right: no-one much pays attention. They're too focused on the roulette and poker tables, which look as if they might be made of real wood — rosewood or mahogany? — not that plastic-looking stuff. The crowd is different. I'm not sure if it's the scotch, martinis and champagne instead of beer, or if it's a general nonchalance. As long as we get some of those generous tips Harry mentioned, I'll be a happy girl.

Our performance is smooth tonight. I've only glitched a couple of times, and it didn't even faze me. Must be the shot of vodka I took at home. Or being tired from work. Or an attitude adjustment after spending hours this week sitting and holding Snap's hand — nothing like the prospect of death to make you wake up to yourself. Priorities.

We're working through the same set list as last time, when Harry angles his head, trying to direct my gaze to someone in the crowd. I'm looking but not seeing. I keep singing, and looking, because he seems agitated that I'm not getting it.

"What?" I whisper during his solo.

He shakes his head, unable to talk and play lead break at the same time. Then it's my turn to sing again. It'd be comical if it weren't so frustrating.

"Joe Davidson," he manages to whisper.

Like I'm supposed to know who that is. Then it clicks: Solway Records – the company Harry does session work for. Oh crap. I'm not ready for this. It's only our second gig. What was Harry thinking? Suddenly my confidence takes a U-turn, and I'm a sea of tight muscles.

It's his turn to solo again. I stand close to him and hiss. "Tonight? Why?"

"I didn't invite him."

"So how?"

"Dunno. Do the new one," he says. And it takes me a moment to realise he's transitioned into an original song we've been working on. I glare. Thanks for the warning.

I try not to look panicked as I search for the lyrics on my iPad. Got them.

As I sing, I scan the crowd, seeing if anyone particular is paying attention. There he is ... maybe? Towards the back of the room, a guy leaning against a pillar, watching us. He's got that middle-aged, paunch-bald thing going on. He must be the only person in the room without a drink; both his hands are tucked into the pockets of his leather jacket. I stumble on a phrase. Crap. I flick my eyes back to my iPad, trying not to look obvious. At least the bit I made up rhymed with the previous line. It's an original. Who's gonna know?

We finish the song and switch back to our normal repertoire. Joe, if it is actually him, keeps staring. My squirm-factor slides up a notch. My dress is clinging in all the wrong places. Sweat prickles my scalp. But he must like us. He's not smiling or anything, but he's still there. He stays for the start of the next song.

I've got to get this under control. Show him we have the talent he's looking for. My singing isn't the problem. I'm rockin' every song. It's what to do with my body that throws me. I need some dance lessons, something that'll give me physical confidence. I attempt a slinky move and think I actually pull it off. There's only fifteen minutes left before we finish our set and get to talk with him. I'm filled with excitement ... and dread. I can imagine the three of us cosied up in a booth, Harry and Joe exchanging testosterone and me sipping a vodka martini, smiling stupidly every now and then, unable to verbalise my horror and enthusiasm at being considered for a recording project.

He's on the move. Maybe he's getting a drink? Nope. He saunters right past the bar and out of the room. I deflate. Why the hell couldn't he stay for another few minutes? All that anticipation for nothing. As soon as Harry and I finish up, I crack it.

"Seriously?"

"What's the problem?"

Harry moves towards the bar, and I follow, desperate to voice my annoyance. "He just walked off."

"So? No-one said there was going to be a meeting. He dropped in of his own volition. He didn't have to."

"Yeah but..." My shoulders slump as I slide onto a bar stool. "I mean, why not at least wave or something?"

"Why? He's not the queen. You've done two gigs and you're expecting royal treatment? He doesn't know you from a bar of soap. Maybe you need to lower your expectations a little."

"Fuck."

"Language."

Crap. Okay, I'm a diva. But this industry is... I hate it and love it at the same time. Is that normal? How do entertainers survive without going crazy? No wonder so many of the brilliant ones die young. It scares me that maybe I want this more than I realise.

Tomorrow, I'll come down from my lofty high and everything will be mundane again. Then I'll visit Snap and remind myself what the real world is like.

Freaking hell. Harry's knock on the car window gives me a start. I've been sitting in here, in Snap's car, pondering whether I'm making the right move. It seems like a good idea. I mean Harry's apartment is nice and cushy with Foxtel and central heating. Who wouldn't like that? But it's Harry's place. And we'll be sharing it for a couple of days before he leaves – his idea – so I can get comfortable with how his stuff works. I mean a washing machine is a washing machine isn't it? It's not like it's What does this button do? Boom!

I wind down the window, and he leans on the doorframe. "Who taught you to park?"

"Snap. Why?"

"Well ... parallel means ... never mind. I thought you were coming a couple of hours ago?"

"Sorry. I thought I'd drop in and see him on the way."

I don't tell him that I was secretly hoping Snap would somehow give me a miraculous sign to let me know if I'm doing the right thing or not. Not a chance. He was still lying there with that hissing machine breathing for him. If I'm honest, I'm pretty sure he would say I was crazy if I didn't go ahead.

"Any change?"

I shake my head.

"Poor kid," Harry says, and there's the flicker of annoyance I get when he uses that word "kid, kiddo". Sometimes he seems like an old man in a young man's body. He thumps the roof of the car. "Pop the boot."

I point to the back seat. "It's just these boxes."

"Oh." He looks surprised.

"You said not to bring bedding and stuff, yeah?" I don't tell him that most of the stuff in our apartment belongs to Snap.

"Yep. All taken care of."

Harry tries to open the rear driver's side door, but it's locked.

"Hang on a minute." I reach behind my headrest and pull on the lock. "Gotta love old cars." Snap's not wrong when he calls it a bomb. A late 1990s silver Honda Civic. But it gets us from A to B in one piece.

Harry yanks the door open and pulls out two of the boxes. I grab a third and we trudge them up to the lobby lift. It feels weird, as if I'm actually moving in with him. Only, he'll be catching a plane to Sydney on Friday to meet his ship. Then I'll have to get used to being in a strange place and working with strange musos.

Harry insists the gigs will round out my experience, get my confidence up, because I can't always stay in my comfort zone working with him – as if the stage is ever a comfortable place for me. Stop. Think positive.

The boxes he's carrying are heavy – my books probably. His face is red by the time the lift doors close. I smile to myself. He's trying to impress me. When we get to his front door, he presses the boxes against the wall for support and tries to reach for his pocket.

"I'll get them," I say.

"Would you mind?"

I put my box down and start digging around in his pants pocket. His face goes redder and so does mine. Awkward. I pull the keys out and unlock the door, propping it open while he lumbers past me down the hallway. I retrieve my box and follow. I pass a little table with a polished wooden dish on it and pause to drop the keys into it. I guess that's where I'm going to be leaving them for the next six weeks. New habits.

He turns right, through a doorway. "You okay?" he calls.

"Yep, right behind you."

He dumps the boxes just inside and moves back into the hallway. "Make yourself at home. I'll get the last one."

I start to object, but he's already gone. I check out the space. I only had a quick glance at it a few days ago, after he first offered it to me. Now it feels way different. Suspiciously fresh. Like everything is shiny and new. The room also seems to come with its own cat. A black and white boofy creature that's sitting on my bed.

"Hello. And who might you be?"

It reminds me of a Boynton cat, with its head looking strangely too small for its plump body. Its intense yellow eyes defy me to dethrone it. I stand hands on hips, hoping an authoritative posture might show it who's boss.

"Where did you come from?"

It licks its fur a couple of times, then curls up, its head resting on its paws, still keeping an eye on me. It wins the staring contest – I relent, sit next to it and stroke its short fur, softer and thicker than I expected. I'm immediately rewarded with a tractor engine purr. It's a nice sensation. The only felines I've known in the past were Samuel's cat, Smith, who didn't like anyone except Samuel; and the farm cats – mean, lean, feral, rat-catching machines that growled if you got too near.

"I see you've met Mr Pink." Harry says. He's hovering in the doorway, holding the last box.

I stand and take it from him, place it on top of one of the others.

Harry points to a chair beside the bed. "May I?"

I shrug. "It's your place." Then it occurs to me, this is my bedroom ... for the time being.

He sits and looks accusingly at the cat. "You traitor, Pink. She's only been here a few minutes, and you've deserted me already."

I return to sitting on the bed. "He's a big smooch. How come I've never met him before?"

"He comes and goes as he feels like it. Usually doesn't venture into the rest of the place. Makes a furry mess of the bedding though. I had to replace it."

Ah, that explains the newness of the doona cover. Mr Pink responds by lifting his back leg and licking his bits.

I laugh. "You have classy friends."

"He's not my friend. I don't actually know who he belongs to. But he's well fed, judging by the stomach on him. I wouldn't recommend leaving any food uncovered in the kitchen. Little bugger helped himself to a hot chicken I left on the bench once. Foil pack and all."

I laugh again and stroke Mr Pink's head. He responds by lifting his chin and closing his eyes. "Mr Pink. That's such a wack name for a beautiful beast like you."

"Wack?"

"You know ... lame." Now I'm thinking how lame I sound, trying to use street-speak from the pub. And my swearing? Harry's still on my back about it. He says I'm above it. That I used to have a better vocabulary. But that was a lifetime ago. Just because he doesn't swear ... actually, now I think about it, not even back in Wineera. Tough. I like swearing. I mean "fuck" – that's a whole world of expression: fuck, fucked, fucking, fuckitty-fuck, fucker. It conveys everything I want to say in one word. Economical, I call it. I'm trying to substitute freakin' for fucking, but I doubt I'll ever get there. Fuck feels so good rolling off my tongue. Crap. Will I ever get the hang of being the "new me" Harry wants? It'd be so much easier just to be the "real me". Fuck it.

"Don't know his real name," Harry says. "But the first time I saw him, he reminded me of Steve Buscemi. You know – the actor from Boardwalk Empire. And Reservoir Dogs. Tarantino. Have you seen the movie? It's a cult classic."

I shake my head. It's probably another one of those ancient Mr Miyagi movies. He was never this retro back in Wineera. Is this part of his new "jazz persona'? I bet he wants me to watch it.

"Dark humour. If you're into that kind of thing, I'll play it for you one night."

Bingo.

He points at Mr Pink. "See how his eyes kind of bulge a little around the edges?"

I can't. Mr Pink's face is buried in his butt again.

"Well ... they do. And he always looks a bit startled. Reminds me of Steve's character in the movie. Mr Pink."

Harry leans forward and rubs Mr Pink's exposed stomach. He's rewarded with a swift belt from a paw. Mr Pink jumps off the bed, struts over to the window and disappears behind a curtain.

"Is that his favourite spot to sit?"

Harry walks over and pushes the curtain aside, revealing a pet door built into the lower section of the window. "Must have been the previous owners. I haven't bothered removing it. I can block it up though, if you don't want a visitor in the middle of the night."

"No, no leave it. He'll be good company while you're away." I stand next to Harry at the window, and I'm surprised to see a decent-sized balcony outside. During rehearsals, I haven't ventured much further than Harry's music room, lounge room, kitchen and toilet.

In the courtyard below, there's a well-maintained grassy common area. "Where the hell does he come from? We're three storeys up."

Harry points to a fourth storey apartment. "Up there, maybe. I've seen him walking along their balcony. Then again, he could just be an opportunist and visit anyone and everyone for food and attention."

"It's dangerous, though. What if he slipped?"

Harry shrugs. "That's Mr Pink for you: a thief who gets away with shit."

"You said shit."

Harry smiles. He's still gazing out the window. I smile too; I must be rubbing off on him. We're standing close, and I catch the scent of musky deodorant and fresh sweat, and there's his dark-blond beard. I want to touch it. To feel if it's soft or scratchy. He looks down, and I'm swept back to another moment, a lifetime ago. The impulse is there to repeat it, but I remember how it ended. Instead, I stand on my toes and peck his cheek. His beard tickles my lips, prickly.

"Thanks. For this," I say. "It means a lot that you trust me."

Harry steps back. "Sure. I'll leave you to unpack. If there's anything you need just holler. I'll go move your car into the parking lot. The tenants next door don't own one, so you can use their spot."

I sit on the vacated bed and run my hand over the doona cover. It's silky and cool. New. He must have bought it especially for me. My tattered boxes look foreign in these polished surroundings, the contents jaded. Maybe I should just throw everything out. Start anew. My old self included.

11

Consanguinity

Her house is a single-fronted weatherboard with a struggling, skeletal magnolia tree crowding the courtyard. Number twenty. Snap's age. I'm still surprised by how easy it was to find her address online. All I did was type in her phone number, and it came up. That just seems wrong. S Gilling.

I rest my hand on her picket gate as I stand shivering. What if she's horrible? What if she gets upset, or breaks down, and I don't know what to do? Come on. I need to deal with it, else stand here and freeze. I should have brought a jacket, but it was warm when I left home.

I lift the catch, expecting it to be stiff because everything about today seems hard, including running out of coffee this morning. The gate glides open. The concrete path is neat and, even though I know it's silly, I'm careful not to step on the dividing cracks – gotta please the good-luck gods today.

There's no screen, no doorbell, just a hefty-looking wooden door that looks as though it'll hurt my knuckles. A radio must be on somewhere down the back of the house, and I wonder if Snap's gran is one of those women who leaves it on as a burglar deterrent when she's out. I rap on a frosted glass pane to the side of the door. There's a scrabbling noise inside, the yapping of a small dog, and muffled shushing. A fuzzy pink figure appears behind the glass.

"Who is it?"

"Mrs Gilling?"

"Yes. Who is it?"

"Hello. I'm a friend of your grandson, Snap... I mean George. Can I speak to you for a minute?"

The woman falls silent, but the dog still barks. She shushes it again. "What do you want?"

"He's had... an accident."

The door opens a fraction. She's solid, short, and her face is soft with undefined features like silly putty. Nothing sleek or cat-like about her. Nothing like Snap. Not even in her youth, I suspect.

"What's happened? Is George okay?"

The greying muzzle of a fox terrier pokes through the gap in the door. The dog snuffles, and the woman pushes it away with her foot. "Get back, Georgie."

Georgie. Really?

"I'm sorry to tell you this, but he's in hospital. He's had a stroke. We don't know if he's going to wake up."

"George? Oh, that's terrible." She blinks.

I have no idea what to say next and even less when she suddenly closes the door in my face. What the hell? I'm conscious my hands have formed fists. I want to bash on her bloody door, yell what a disgrace of a grandmother she is, but then there's the metal-on-metal sliding sound of a door chain, and the door opens again.

"You better come in."

She stands back for me to enter, then pushes one of those sausage draft stoppers against the back of the door as she closes it. "What did you say your name was?"

"Lauren."

"You know his mother's passed on? It's just me and little Georgie now." Georgie gives a yap at the mention of his name. "Come on, I'll put the kettle on. I'm Shirley."

I follow her shuffling progress, which is aided by a walking stick. The hallway has an elaborately patterned carpet runner, and we pass a couple of bedrooms with floral bedspreads and antique-looking furniture. Her lounge room is at the back of the house, next to the kitchen. She motions me forward. "Take a seat." Her furniture is covered in those multi-coloured woollen rugs made up of crochet squares, just like I imagine a grandma's house ought to look. There's a real fire going in the grate, not one of those fake gas things. I make a beeline for the recliner next to it. For a moment it takes me back to Wineera, Samuel's house, and something sharp pinches in my chest.

Shirley disappears into the kitchen for a few minutes, then returns with a plate of sliced Swiss roll — the jam variety. She passes it to me. "Here you go. Tuck in. Tea won't be a minute."

I'd kill for a coffee, but I'm afraid she'll probably have something thrifty like International Roast. When did I become such a snob? She goes back to the kitchen, accompanied by the sound of Georgie's paws tapping on the tiles. He whines as Shirley chatters to him over her tea-making. This can't be the same grandmother Snap mentioned. She's too sweet.

Shirley returns, carrying a tray with cups and a cosied teapot, her walking stick hooked over one arm. Her hands shake with the effort, and I reach to grab the tray as her foot catches on a rug. She pauses to take a breath, steady herself, and I put the tray on a little table in front of the fire.

"Thank you," she says, collapsing into the armchair opposite me. She looks relieved to be off her feet. "Tell me. George is here in Melbourne? Is he in a bad way? Where's his father?"

"Yes, George is here. We're not sure how he his. He's still unconscious. His dad is back home."

"Ah, so you're from Wineera too?"

I nod, tell her everything I know, watching her carefully. She's hard to read, saying nothing until I mention the hospital has tried to call. Then she looks embarrassed.

"It's a new answering machine. I have no idea how to use it, so I ended up turning the sound off. It's always telemarketers anyway."

She smiles, and I notice how her pink lipstick looks a little lopsided. I guess she can't see well enough to apply it evenly.

A thought seems to suddenly occur to her. "You're not his girlfriend?"

I hesitate. Snap made it clear early on she never accepted him being gay. I should probably shut up, but I've come this far without him knowing, I may as well go the whole hog. "No. Just a good friend."

"Oh, he's still a poof then?" She chuckles, making a little snuffling noise, and I'm reminded of that saying – how owners often reflect their pets.

I want to laugh – the word "poof" coming out of her lady-like mouth like that. "Um. Yes. That's not likely to change. I mean, it's who he is, no choice really. Is there?"

I wait to see how she responds to my challenge. She leans forward to pat Georgie, then pours the tea.

I fill the awkward silence.

"So, George lived here when he was little?" I ask.

She nods as she busies herself with milk and sugar. "Yes. After his mother got sick."

She hands me a cup, then gets up and moves to the fireplace. There's a trinket box on the mantelpiece, which looks like redwood. She takes it down and strokes the lid. "Melissa. Well, what's left of her. I scattered the rest under the rose bushes in the back garden."

"I'm sorry." I struggle for what else to say.

She replaces the box and sits again. Georgie jumps up and rests his wiry head on her lap. Her hand automatically rubs his back.

"George's dad wouldn't let him come to the funeral. Said he was too young. I think it's a shame. It was a beautiful service. We had a big row over it."

"I'm sorry."

"Demitrius hasn't come?"

I assume she means Snap's dad. "No, like I said, he's back in Wineera. He's in a wheelchair, Snap... George says. Some sort of accident."

"Good riddance to that fucker, I say."

I nearly choke. Shirley smirks and taps her head. Grey roots show beneath her brown curls. "Something wrong upstairs with that one. Joined a religious cult after he married my Mel. He wanted to move Mel and Georgie to America. Then Mel got sick."

"So, she moved in here, with you?"

She nods. "Watching your own child die is the worst thing a parent can endure."

"It must have been awful."

"Yes, it was. That mongrel didn't even want her to have pain relief. Some religious mumbo jumbo. I couldn't let her suffer like that. Not for months on end. No mother could." Her face sags with the memory. "I had to help her."

It's on the tip of my tongue to ask what happened, but if I do, it'll break the spell. Instead, I squish a piece of cake into my mouth, and listen. Georgie's eyes follow my motion, and I have this insane picture of a thought bubble over his head: Are you going to eat all of that?

Shirley is staring into the fire, oblivious, her mouth pursed. "Death is a strange animal. It makes you do things you never thought you could."

I'm too frightened to ask what she means, and I wonder if she even realises what she's saying, to me, a stranger. Then I think of Mum wasting away in the hospice. Would someone "help" her eventually? Would I be brave enough to?

"Demitrius went off his rocker after Mel died. Took George. Broke my heart when he won custody."

"So, you wanted to keep George?"

Shirley looks at me as though I'm crazy. "Of course. I loved that little tyke. But Demitrius wouldn't let me see him. When they moved away, I started sending money. He didn't refuse it. I only hope George got some benefit from it."

"And ... it doesn't bother you that George is gay?"

Shirley stares at me for the longest time. "He's blood."

Later, as I'm standing on her porch, saying an awkward goodbye, I notice the magnolia tree's twiggy branches are budding. Strange for this time of year. I read once that sometimes, old trees can suddenly, and madly, blossom in their dying throes.

12

Divulgence

Fish and chips. "Mmm." I suck the last bit of salty grease from my thumb. So good. A picnic rug on Harry's lounge room floor, a good feed of junk food in our stomachs, and French champagne. An impromptu birthday party.

Harry tips the last dribble into my glass. "That's it for that one."

"Ta. I'm still annoyed. I can't believe I forgot. I would have organised something nicer for you. A night out with your muso mates maybe?"

"You've got enough on your plate. I'll catch up with them when I get back. This is good. Plush carpet, cushions, crystal. The candles are a nice touch."

"Ripped paper, sauce bottle, paper towels. You're turning twenty-one. You deserve something better."

"Like what?"

"I don't know ... lobster?"

"Do you like lobster?"

"Mmm, not really, but we wouldn't have to eat it, we could just look at it."

"Spell profligate."

"I don't even know what that means. Oh. Wait!" I get up and run to my bedroom. When I return, I settle next him and hold out my hand. "Look." It's the tiny dictionary he gave me as a parting gift. "Immoral. Wasteful. Nice."

He takes the dictionary from me and flips through its miniature pages. "You kept it?"

"Of course."

He's looking at me with a sexy smile, and now I'm embarrassed. I point to his glass. "Another bottle?"

"Pass. Early flight tomorrow. But you go ahead."

"No. I'm fine," say. It's probably not a good idea. I've only had two glasses to his three, but it's hitting me hard. Still, I don't care. I need to unwind. Between visiting Snap, my job and learning a bunch of new songs so I can do gigs with other musos after Harry leaves for his cruise, I'm dead on my feet. So, so freakin' tired. I could fall asleep right where I'm sitting. I hold up my glass. There's a tiny swish of bubbles in the base.

"Another toast. This one's to you and me surviving more than three months without killing each other."

"Has it only been that long?" he says.

I poke out my tongue. He's right: it seems longer, more than months – maybe years. No, not years. I'm drunk. God, I wish life would slow down, even a fraction. It's too much. I'm a character in one of those flipbook stories, where drawings whip into life with each flick of a page. A boy in my class at school used to make them, only his were all about boobs and dicks.

"To hump month." he says.

We chink glasses.

"Let's see if we make it to seven," I say.

He screws up his face. "Isn't that years? Seven-year itch or something?"

"Whatever. Months, years. Same thing."

We settle into a quiet comfortableness, and I think my brain finally switches off. This is what it must be like to be a guy, when they do that not-thinking thing. I like it.

"Hey." Harry kicks my foot. "While I'm away you should visit Freda. See a movie together, or something."

"Like I don't have enough on my plate." There's a hint of sarcasm in my voice.

"It'll do you good. Get your mind off things. Have a girls night out."

I kind of like the idea: a thirty-something girlfriend – not a mother figure – who isn't all about boys, clothes, make-up and tweeting gossip. Someone with life experience who isn't going to lecture me or make me feel like a kid if I ask about awkward stuff. Someone who doesn't know me and doesn't give a crap about my past. But there's her intuitive thing. That's plain weird.

"She's a bit scary."

Harry laughs. "You'll be fine."

Secretly, I think she's kinda cool, in a freaky way. I wonder if Freda can teach me how to read people. It'd be awesome to tap into that kind of thing. That's if it's not hereditary or something. Listen to me. I'll be riding unicorns next. I shuffle my butt across the floor until I can lean against the couch. Harry joins me. "That's better," he says. "My back was killing me."

Side by side, we sit looking at the empty fireplace. We should have lit it. It's cold enough, and it'd be nice to have flames to stare at, to mesmerise us. But I don't mention it because, at this moment, it might bring up a conversation I don't want to have. A memory of another fireplace I've tried so hard to put behind me. Still, something is eating at me.

I want to know what Harry knows, what he thinks. What might be waiting for me back in Wineera. Blame?

"You've surprised me, you know," Harry says.

"Hmm?"

"You're a lot stronger than I've given you credit for."

"What do you mean?"

"Snap. You're there for him. No matter what."

"He'd do the same for me."

"You sure?"

"Hell, yes. He's supported me from the start. Helped me get a job, found somewhere for us to live, taught me not to take crap from anyone. He's had my back. And besides, I'm the whole reason he's in hospital. If he hadn't spoken up for me, it wouldn't have happened." I cross my arms and add, "Though I never asked him to."

"You don't know that. It sounded like that douche already had an issue with Snap being gay."

Harry shuffles closer, and heat blossoms where our shoulders connect. Oh, how I'm craving for that fireplace to distract us. Suddenly Harry's finger is tracing the back of my hand. "No-one's ever thrown me a fish and chip party."

My heart. How can one small touch, skin on skin, be so loaded with sensitivity? It's enticing, but strange. Scary. I pull my hand away, overwhelmed. What's going on with him? A week ago, he said we were all business, nothing else. Now he's getting all up close. Too close.

"I guess fish and chips are pretty original for a twenty-first. Are your parents going to give you a proper one? When are they back?" I feel as if I'm making conversation for the sake of it, ignoring what's really going on.

"Who knows? They're more into saving the world." There's an aftertaste of bitterness in his words.

"Huh."

"Huh? I'm sensing disapproval," he says.

I wave my arm to encompass the room. "Look around. Look at what you've got. And you think your parents don't care?"

"They care. They care about lots of people. That's what they do. You know they sponsored Freda as a child? Helped her come to Australia? She's effectively my big sister."

"That's so cool."

"Yeah. They're generous souls. Always volunteering for worthy projects. For other people."

"Huh."

"Again, with the huh?"

"Where exactly are they?"

"Who knows? Everywhere they're needed except here."

"You're being a big baby."

He laughs. "Maybe. It'd just be nice to know someone is there for you." He takes my hand and holds it in both of his. "Like you're there for Snap."

There's that tingle again. "Like I said—"

"I'm going to miss you," he murmurs.

And there goes my heart again. Why do I want to be near him but further away at the same time? He's watching me. Too closely. His breath is savoury with wine and salt. He squeezes my hand. "I need to tell you something."

I tense. I knew something was going on. I'm just not sure I want to know what it is.

"And now comes the hard part," he adds.

I turn to look at him. "What do you mean?"

"The part where you either hate me or forgive me."

Now I'm scared, but I'm too tired and tipsy to imagine what might come next. Please don't be something awful. Something that's going to ruin everything. Life feels too fragile right now.

"Promise you won't get mad."

"At what?" I try to move away so I can see his face clearly, but his grip tightens. Is it that bad he thinks I'm going to run away? I steel myself.

"It's about home."

There it is. Nightmare City. The inevitable has raised its ugly head. He's right to hold onto me. All I can do is pretend this isn't happening.

"I'm just going to say it, okay?"

I nod. Get it over with.

"I didn't find you by accident."

"What?" I purse my lips, wait. Everything I've been trying to avoid is looming, like an ominous, unstoppable wave. And I can't outrun it because my legs are in one of those dreams where you're all weighty and cumbersome.

"You know Gran volunteers at the hospice where your mum is. I mean you left a message for Gran as well, right?"

I nod.

"Well, she managed to track the number. I mean, who else would be calling from Melbourne? It wasn't hard to find the pub. She sent me to find you. She's been worried sick."

I can't look at him. My voice trembles. "Are you going to dob me in?"

"For what?"

I bite my lip. "The house," I whisper.

"Are you kidding?"

I stare at the fireplace. It's cold, empty but it's not hard to imagine the flames. An ember falling out, the carpet catching alight ...

"Lauren, it was an accident. You don't blame yourself, do you?"

"But I—"

"It wasn't your fault. It was the chimney. A blockage, maybe a bird's nest or something. Gran told the police she was helping you clean up, burning some old papers in the fireplace."

"She did that?"

"God, Lauren. You should have stayed. You hurt Gran so much. She cares a lot about you."

My throat clenches. "I'm sorry."

I've got my eyes closed now, tears brimming. I'm trying to weigh everything up in my head: consequences, possibilities, the law, Snap, Harry. I can't think.

"It's okay," he says. "You're fine. Don't stress. You're not in trouble."

He lets go of my hand and puts an arm around me, drawing me in. I let him. I'm still trying to absorb everything he's said. "I'm sorry for not coming clean," he says. "But when I saw you in the pub you looked thrown, panicked. I was surprised you even agreed to meet me later. I thought I'd frightened you off. You did almost make a run for it. Remember? You were grabbing your bag when I met you in the café?"

He kisses my forehead, grazing my nose with the roughness of his beard. "I wanted to tell you sooner, but things got too far down the track. And now ..." He takes my hand again, threads his fingers through mine. "I've grown feelings for you ... and I don't want to start anything with a lie between us."

Oh hell. I'm snotting all down my face. Where's his hanky when I need it? I pull myself lose and wipe my nose on a paper towel.

"You okay?" he asks.

I nod, blow my nose, then rest my hands in my lap, stare at them. I'm lost. There's so much to take in. "I'm so stupid. This is the moment I've been dreading. And it seems ridiculous. All that worry eating at me, all this time, for nothing."

"You're not stupid," he says. "You were sixteen and scared, dealing with Samuel's suicide. And your mum wasn't there for you ... and neither was I."

"That wasn't your fault."

"Yes, it was. You deserved better. I could have been there, if I'd really wanted to." He lifts my chin. "You hear me? You deserve better."

I sniff. He doesn't know what I deserve. Doesn't know I would still have run. Doesn't know everything. That I couldn't stay in that town.

"You are amazing," he says.

"I am?"

"And beautiful."

I laugh. "I'm a mess." I wipe my nose again.

"Yes, you are," he says. "You're beautiful. I can't believe I never told you that."

I'm blushing, heat in my cheeks. He's staring. I'm staring back. His gaze drops to my mouth. I've never wanted to be kissed so much, and yet so not. I hug him to avoid the moment, but his mouth reaches a sensitive spot on my neck instead, and I shiver.

"I could get used to this," he whispers.

"What? Fish and chips?"

His chuckle is muted by his mouth against my skin. "Us."

I can't answer. My breath has disappeared somewhere. I want to join it. Escape.

"I wish you were coming with me," he murmurs.

"Me too."

Then he's kissing me, his mouth is warm and salty. I'm responding, as if this is what I've been missing, needing, craving. There's us and nothing but us. He reaches behind me, positions a cushion on the floor, and eases me back. I let myself go. His mouth is back on my neck, his hand on my chest, and something stirs in me. Something deep. My breath quickens. Is this longing? Is this what lust feels like? Whatever it is, it's urgent, needy, and I want him closer, even though I can't believe I'm doing this. But if it's to happen with anyone, I'm glad it's Harry. If I trust anyone, it's him.

But as the weight of his body presses on me, my body suddenly changes tack. The longing strengthens, tightens, deep down in my stomach ... and switches to nausea.

"Stop!"

"What's wrong?"

I push him off and scramble to my feet. "I need some water."

"Lauren?"

I flee to the kitchen, put my palms flat on the cool stone bench-top and rest my forehead on it, waiting for the heat to dissipate. What's wrong with me? It's as though my body is rejecting everything my mind and heart wants.

My mobile rings from the lounge room. I listen to Harry's voice, muted by the walls between us, then turn to grab a glass as the soft thud of his socked feet draws closer, up the hallway.

"Lauren?" He's in the kitchen doorway now. "Are you okay?"

"Yep." I nod, gulping water.

"It's the hospital," he says, holding up my phone.

Vertigo hits, blood draining from my face, my limbs. No-one calls this time of night unless it's bad news.

Harry's smile is tentative. "He's woken up."

13

Recrudescence

The taxi is quick to arrive. I grab my purse and jacket. Harry says he feels bad he's not driving me. I tell him he's drunk too much, and it's wet outside. "Besides, you need to get some sleep. You've got an early start tomorrow. Don't wait up for me."

As I open the front door, he touches my arm. "Wait. Tell me you're okay."

I turn back and look him in the eye. "I'm okay. We're okay. Just ... later."

He nods.

I hold my bag over my head to fend off the rain while I run for the taxi. We drive through dark, slick roads, streetlights refracting in the water drops on my window, like so many diamonds. I'm trying not to think about what's just happened, but my mind is playing back a film-reel of moments, snippets of words, movements, touches, trying to decipher the meaning of it all. Snap. Think about Snap. I hope the crappy weather isn't a bad omen – that Snap is still in one piece, his mind whole.

It's after hours at the hospital, so I have to press an intercom button to gain entry. I hug my jacket close. Freakin' autumn. It was warm yesterday. A voice that sounds as busy as hell answers the intercom, and I'm buzzed through.

Snap's room seems different: there's a static motionless about it. His chest rising and falling is the only movement, and even that seems shallow. It's then I realise they've removed his noisy breathing tube. Now he's got one of those thin, spaghetti-like oxygen tubes wrapped around his ears, the little nubs positioned under his nostrils. The light above his bed is on, and his blankets have been folded down a little to free his arms. That's new too.

I stand beside him, just watching for a moment. His bandages have been removed, and there's a bald patch on the right side of his head with an arc of spidery black stitches, which start in front of his right ear and curve above his forehead.

His eyebrows twitch. Both his eyes open. He's looking at me, expressionless.

"Hi, stranger," I whisper.

He looks puzzled, and when he tries to speak his voice sticks. He grimaces, making a claggy noise as he clears his throat. I hold his hand, trying to encourage him. When he finally speaks, his voice is hoarse and his words are slurred, dragged out.

"Whooo yooo?"

I'm startled even though I've been warned this might happen. But as I stand dumbly petrified, a slow smile spreads across the half of his face that still works.

"Yorrr hair's mmmess," he says.

"You bastard." I lean across his chest and awkwardly hug him. His arms feel frail, like a child's, clinging to my back. A funny gurgling noise comes from his chest, and I realise he's laughing while I'm crying. I extract myself, and he gives a rattly cough.

I try to sort out my hair with my fingers. "You don't look so good yourself, you know," I say.

He half-shrugs, and I regret the words because he really does look terrible.

"Maaake a goood exi ..."

I frown, trying to figure out what he's saying. "A good what?"

"Exxxiii."

"Exit?"

He nods.

"Ah, I get you." I chuckle. "You made the best exit ever! Do you remember the last thing you said to me?"

He shakes his head.

"You said, and I quote, "I am not camp, I am dramatic.""

He gurgle-laughs again.

"How are you feeling? Your chest sounds terrible."

"Fffkin hung-reee."

I laugh, taking a seat by his side. "Not surprising. You've been living on soup through a tube the past couple of weeks. I pick up his call button. "Pizza with the lot?"

"Nooo! Wwwatching myyyy waaayt."

I'm in awe of his humour; his body is gaunt. He tries to lift his arm again, to wave a finger at me, and it takes all his effort, he's drained.

"Well, some tea might have to do for now," I say. "Maybe some cheese and bickies if they can dig them up."

He crinkles his nose. "Iiiced VoVos or noth-th-th-thing."

"Princess."

I squeeze his hand.

It's around eleven-thirty. The rain has stopped. Harry must have gone to bed and left the hall light on for me. His suitcase is sitting just inside the front door. I hang up my jacket and look down the corridor. His door is open, and there's a soft glow coming from his beside lamp.

I stand in his doorway and whisper, "Harry? Are you awake?"

He doesn't respond. He's lying on his stomach, head resting on one arm. I should turn his lamp off. I slip off my shoes and pad over to his bed. He sighs and rolls onto his side. The sheet falls away to his hip, revealing the strength of his wide chest, the honey blond hair on his arms, his narrow waist. Beautiful. It's so tempting to reach over and touch his skin, to trace the slope of his shoulder down to his hip, feel the structure of his bones and muscles underneath. I don't. He looks vulnerable, and I'm a creep for watching him without his knowledge. I click his lamp off, pull his door closed and head back down the hall to take a shower.

The pelting water feels good, the night's tension oozing away. I squeeze my eyes shut and let the water spray on my face, my hair, my shoulders. I soap my body, enjoying the slipperiness on my skin, on my breasts. And I think of Harry, imagining him pressing me up against the shower wall, his hands gripping my waist, his mouth on mine, then slipping down to my neck, kissing me where he did earlier tonight, on that tender spot that made me shiver, his hands sliding lower.

Suddenly, it's Samuel in my head. The smell of him, the heaviness of him, the grunts and ugliness of that night. I pull my arms to my chest, tight, protective, nausea returning. Why is my memory betraying me? That night is supposed to be buried. Deep. Is this what's going to happen now? Every time I get close to someone?

I spin the hot water tap off and brace myself as the shock of the cold water drains away the nightmare. Shivering, I turn the hot back on, waiting for my body to stop shaking.

Eventually I get out, wrap myself in a towel and sit on the side of the bath. I need to get a grip. This is my body. My life. Maybe there's only one way forward.

Harry is oblivious to me standing next to his bed. I drop my towel, lift his bedcovers and ease in beside him.

He stirs. "What—"

"Shhh."

We lie there, side by side, breathing in the almost-dark. Each one of my heartbeats punctuates a second. Thud. Thud. Thud. We're so still I wonder if Harry's fallen asleep again.

"What's going on?" he whispers. "I thought you didn't—"

"I changed my mind. Is that okay?"

I reach for his face, my fingertips landing on the smoothness of his forehead, then running down to the roughness of his cheek and beard. He shifts, and I catch the glimmer of his eyes. It's weird, the presence of someone else's body, warm, so close. Weird ... and terrifying.

Harry pulls back, takes my hand. "Maybe we should talk first."

"Can you just hold me?" My voice breaks. "Please?"

He props himself up and leans to turn on his lamp.

"No! Leave it off."

"What is it? What's happened?"

"It's nothing... I just need you to hold me."

"Lauren—"

"Please?"

His weight shifts, and I lift my head so he can push an arm under me. My hair catches under his elbow. "Ow." Even my laugh is tense.

"Sorry."

"It's okay."

He strokes my face. "Is it Snap?"

I shake my head. "He's fine."

I can't say any more. If I speak, a torrent of words will bleed me dry. The muscles in my throat contract. It hurts. Can a person die from keeping so much inside?

I should tell him. Everything. Just let it out. Let it breathe. It wouldn't be so bad, would it? It was something that happened to me. It isn't who I am now. It wasn't my fault. Maybe telling him, telling anyone, might make it go away. Like bursting a blister ... all that's inside let loose, and the pressure gone.

But what if he's revolted by it? Or worse, what if he feels sorry for me? I couldn't bear to see sympathy in his eyes, for him to treat me like something broken, something too delicate to live an ordinary life.

I can't think about it. Not now. Not with Harry so close.

I wait, holding my breath. Finally, he kisses me. His tongue warm, still a little salty, beard soft, grazing my skin. My hand rests on his chest, fingers brushing the few coarse hairs that curl there. I have the strangest sensation of floating, like I'm losing myself. He's still kissing me, and I press myself against him, waiting for that feeling to return – the one from earlier: the longing, the physical needing. It should be part of this. And ... I want to feel it. But then he reaches for my butt cheek, pulls my hips to his, and his hardness is there, between us, pressing against my thigh.

I freeze. Can't move. Can't breathe.

I want to scream, but my throat has closed. I'm looking up at Harry, above me, his face concerned. He's speaking, but I can't hear him. Now he's shaking me, tapping my cheek and ... I'm back.

"Lauren? What's wrong?" he's saying. "What happened? You scared me."

"I don't know."

I look down at my nakedness, throw my hands over my face. The shame. The excruciating shame. I can't face him. Can't face it.

It's just after 6 am. Harry is in the shower. He'll be leaving to catch his plane for the cruise soon. I could stay here, in my own bed. Hide. Like I did last night, when he followed me and knocked on my door, calling to me. And I told him to go away, I was fine.

Will he try to come in now? Try to talk to me? It'll be better if I get up and make some coffee. Pretend like nothing's happened.

But he's leaving. Six weeks. I can't let him go without explaining. It wouldn't be fair. And if I don't, it'll be even more awkward when he comes back. Maybe he'll just think I'm a nutcase and leave me be. I could live with that. But I know he's smarter than that. Kinder.

I roll over under my doona. There's a clunk at the window, and Mr Pink comes wandering in. He jumps onto my bed, his heavy paws sinking into my stomach as he strolls up to nuzzle my nose.

I'll stay here. It'll be easier.

But then I hear Harry turn the water off. The dull clunk of the shower door. The memory of my own shower last night returns. Why is it all coming back now? I want it to go away. Leave me alone. It's done with.

Mr Pink is kneading my stomach. I wait for him to stop, to step off me, turn his three circles, then settle by my side. He doesn't. He keeps kneading.

Okay. Coffee. It's always the answer.

I stand with arms crossed at the kitchen sink, looking out the window, waiting for the coffee machine to do its gurgly thing. It's raining again.

"Morning."

The thud of Harry's carry bag on the floor makes me jump. I keep my back to him, shoulders tense. "Morning. Coffee?"

"No time. I'll get some at the airport." He comes up behind me. "Lauren?" He touches my shoulder. "You okay?"

I swallow, turn, and before I know it, I'm pressing myself onto his chest, sniffling. He hugs me, and it's exactly what I need. Face buried, I mumble. "I am now."

He doesn't say anything, just holds me until I'm ready to let go. I want to stay here. All day. But he has to leave. When I eventually pull away, he releases me, and I reach for some paper towel to wipe my nose, then stand back, arms crossed again. "Sorry."

"Don't be."

He's frowning, fringe hanging in front of his worried eyes. Beautiful eyes. I want to reach up, brush his hair aside, but instead I curl my fingers, pull my arms tighter. Awkward. He obviously doesn't know what to say and neither do I.

"Want to talk?"

I shake my head. "Later. You have to go. Can't miss your plane."

"I feel bad leaving you like this. I was really worried about you last night."

"Don't be. I'm okay. I promise. I need to work through some stuff. It's not you. I just need to ... take things slower, you know?"

"K," he says. "We can do that." Then as an afterthought he adds, "How's Snap?"

I brighten and manage a smile that's not an effort. "Doing well. He's awake, eating, talking ... well, slurring for now. The doctor says there's a good chance of a full recovery, but we have to wait and see."

"That's fantastic."

"Yep."

Another awkward moment before Harry bridges the silence. "Listen, you know how I mentioned Freda last night? I was thinking... she studied law before she became an artist. She might have some useful contacts for Snap. I mean if he wants to press charges against Bob, now that he's—"

I clear my throat. "Sure. That would be great. I don't know what he wants to do yet, but I'll follow up with her."

"She's good to talk to," he adds.

"Uh huh." I know what he's saying.

"And this," he reaches on top of the fridge, finds a piece of cut-out newspaper and shows it to me. "It's an audition notice for a stage show."

"But—"

He presses it into my hand. "Just look at it. Okay? I'd love to stay and argue with you, because I know you want to, but it's a good idea to explore all bases. A recording deal may never come through. It's good to spread your wings. Try different things. You can't sit around like some princess waiting for her fairy godmother to fly in on a broom. Speaking of flying, I gotta."

He's pauses, as though he's wants to say something more.

I know what he needs. "We're okay. We'll talk when you get back. About everything."

"Sure?"

"Sure."

I take his shoulders, spin him around and give him a push. "Anyway, you're getting your fairies and witches confused. Go on. Get out of here. Up, up and away with you."

He grabs his carry bag, and I follow him down the hallway. It's freezing outside. I pull my dressing gown closer. He's still hesitating, suitcase in hand, as if he's unable to find his words.

"Look," I say, "I got a bit emotional is all. I shouldn't have ..." I take a breath, smile brightly. "We'll talk. I promise. I'm okay. And we're all good." I reach up, kiss his cheek. Everything – my fear, my longing, my need for him to understand and not push – is showing in my eyes. I know it.

He leans in and kisses my forehead, then grabs me tight, squeezing. "Take care of you." He heads off down the landing, turning back to smile before he slips around the corner towards the lift.

I listen to the receding rumble of his suitcase wheels, then close the door. There's an immediate sense of emptiness to the apartment, so I fetch my coffee and go in search of Mr Pink. I find him dozing on the lounge where the sun is filtering through the blinds. Cheeky thing thinks he can take over the house now that the boss is gone. I sit and pet him. He hardly stirs. Comfortable. Confident. I could learn from him.

What do cats think about?

Thinking. It's a dangerous thing. "But we won't go there, will we, Mr Pink?"

"Murr."

"No need to dig up old stuff, good and buried, hey?" Still, my mind edges there.

I wanted to be with Harry. Why wouldn't my body let me? I refuse to believe that one night out of all my years – one horrible night – could still be affecting me so much. That's just stupid. It must have been first-time nerves. Because it was a first. Samuel doesn't count. That wasn't the same thing. And Harry would never, ever ...

I mean, what's there to stress about? I'm not being blamed for the house fire anymore. Never was, turns out. So, everything is fine. It should be a relief. But it's not. And I'm thinking it's the guilt, the tension, that's been keeping me afloat all this time. So now I'm in freefall. Everything has changed, and my mind is still catching up. That makes so much sense. That's what last night was all about – nothing to do with Samuel after all. God. What a relief.

"Okay, that's enough," I tell Mr Pink. "We've sorted it."

I look about the room. It's going to be weird, having the place to myself. Even though I've been in every room in the apartment now, I've never pried. It didn't feel right. It doesn't now, but the temptation is there, to open drawers, sneak peeks at Harry's private things. I should resist. He trusts me. And trust is so fragile.

14

Frangible

Intimidated is the word, I think. Outside the café window, I watch Freda moving between tables, serving the breakfast crowd and connecting effortlessly. Confident as. Is that a result of her special talent? She's still wearing the little peasant handkerchief thing on her head, looking girlish.

As if sensing my presence, she looks up and catches me staring. She smiles and waves me inside, moving towards the door. Now I have no choice. "Come, come," she says. "I will take a brcak. We can have coffee. Or hot chocolate. You prefer chocolate?"

We sit in the same window booth as last time. "Lucky seat," she says.

I smile, unsure of what she means.

"Love birds seat," she adds.

Huh. Maybe she's not so astute after all.

"You and Harry. You are living together now, yes?"

I'm not really paying attention; I'm mesmerised by her smoky eyes and thick accent. "Um, no. I'm minding his apartment."

She smiles as if she's indulging a child in a lie. "Call it what you want."

Already, she's making me pissy, stirring an impulse to explain, defend myself. "Just until he gets back. From his cruise."

Her expression doesn't change. "Lauren," she says, "why don't you let life be? Go with the flow, as they say. It's much easier to accept what is. Less energy. More joy."

I give her a sideways look. "What is this? Dr Phil?"

She holds up her hands. "Okay, we can pretend if you like."

God, she's so annoying. It's like she already knows what's in my soul, already knows my secrets, and she's waiting – with the endless patience of a trickle of water weathering a mountain – for me to know it too. And would that be such a bad thing? A tiny, hopeful corner of my mind sparks. But another part, an overwhelming part, says if I even nudge the stone blocking the entrance to that cave, a darkness of memories will unfurl and swallow me. I can't risk it. "I'm not pretending."

She stands. "Something to eat?"

I nod. Any distraction will do. "The muffins look good."

She leaves and my mind stews. Now that I know I'm not being blamed for the house fire, there's no reason I can't go back home to visit Mum. Poor Mum. I picture her, still sitting in that chintz chair, staring out the window. Staring, staring. She hardly knew who I was back then. How is she now? Would it be upsetting for her to see me again? Has she aged even more? And Mary with her cankles – I can't help smiling. Her back porch. The fruit trees and overripe tomatoes. And bam! She's rushing around the side of the house, Samuel's suicide letter in hand. My stomach cramps as the cold stone stirs.

Freda returns with our food and drinks. I tuck in as if I'm starved. If I don't, she'll pick up on my energy and start asking more questions. "I haven't got around to stocking Harry's fridge yet," I tell her. "You'd think working in a convenience store I'd be rolling in food, but my boss doesn't give us any staff discounts. Miser."

"So, are you in love with my little brother?"

I blink. Say what you think, why don't you? I take a sip of hot chocolate to deflect my surprise. She's not going to give up, so I hit back. "I don't know. Love isn't on my agenda at the moment."

She narrows her eyes. "Lauren."

The way she says my name, just the one word, carries so much weight, I'm compelled to answer. Truthfully. "I like him. A lot."

"Good," she says. "You said on the phone you need some help? Yes?"

I nod. "Not me. My friend, Snap. You met him a week or so ago. He needs some legal advice, you know? Or contacts in the legal world or something."

She listens as I relay the situation: how Snap is thinking of pressing charges against Bob, how the police say Bob wants to press charges against Snap, how there were no witnesses to his bashing, and now Snap might be permanently disabled. I pause. "What do you think?"

Her face is blank. "You haven't said what the argument was about."

"Is it important?"

"I don't know. Is it?"

And here's that creepy feeling again, that she does know. How do you protect yourself against someone like this? I cross my arms. "Okay, how do you do that?"

She doesn't even try to pretend. "It's not what you think. I'm not special, there's no magic here."

"Then how?"

It's her turn to reveal something. She tells me about her childhood in Romania, in the early nineties, growing up in an orphanage. "I was lucky," she says. "I was eight when my parents died. Old enough to own my spirit."

I think of my dad dying and my mum being so ill. I'm on the verge of telling her we have something in common, but I suspect she already knows. I press my lips together.

"I learned quickly," she continues. "Get smart or get starved, or sick, or dead." She describes removing clothing from children who had died overnight. Their small bodies limp in her hands. The rows and rows of babies growing into unsocialised children with vacant eyes, incapable of speech. "I would not be like them. I would not let that place break me. I watched. I learned. People are not difficult to read." Her eyes look far away, as if she's back there.

"But I spent four years in that horror, until Harry's parents rescued me. All the Westerners, they wanted babies, babies, babies. But Harry's parents, they were different. They knew my chances were none – a twelve-year-old girl who could not forget or pretend she had no other life. And I was twice as lucky. Romania changed the adoption laws soon after and less help came."

"They adopted you?"

"Not quite. They sponsored me. I was put with a good family there. They gave money for my education, for living, until I am old enough to come to Australia, for myself."

"And that's what made you want to study law? To help other people?"

She laughs. "I was naïve. The law is not for helping. It is for manipulation."

"So, you chose to serve people here instead?"

She shakes her head and laughs again. "What is this notion of "serving" you have? I am not Mother Teresa. Nourishment and friendly words. Often it is all the help people need. And they are happy to pay for it."

I go back to my coffee because my soul is shrinking a little – me and my pathetic problems.

Her voice softens. "And you? What is this pain you carry with such conviction?"

"Conviction?"

"Perhaps I have the wrong word? Let's see ... connection ... correction. No, conviction is right. You are a martyr."

"I am not!"

"Yes."

She says it so simply and with such conviction I believe her. Maybe I am what she says. Has my pain become who I am?

"Who hurt you?" she asks.

"No-one." It's an instinctive response. I chew my lip for a moment. Make a decision. She's not going to stop until I give her something. "Someone ... who shouldn't have."

"Shouldn't have? Nobody should hurt you, Lauren."

"I mean, somebody I trusted."

"Ah trust. There's an old saying, something like "It is those you are closest to who will hurt you the most." Why are you protecting him?"

"I'm not."

She tilts her head, her cynicism so easy to read.

I lower my head and mumble. "I don't think he meant to hurt me. I think he just couldn't control himself."

"Lauren. Look at me." She tilts my face up. "What this man is thinking is one thing. What this man is doing is another. We cannot always control our thoughts. We can control our actions. Do you understand?"

What this man did. I'm tempted to correct her tenses, but I don't. I nod. Though I'm not sure I'm convinced. There were things I could have done differently. Maybe I shouldn't have got so close.

"What this man did. It was not your fault. Okay?"

God, she's scary. I nod again. Then I bite my lip, chewing on a question that's been gnawing at me. We've gone there now. I may as well ask. "Freda?"

"Yes?"

"Should I forgive him?"

Freda falls silent. Have I thrown her? She lifts her head, takes a long slow breath, then sighs before finally looking me in the eye. "Who is this forgiveness for?"

I don't understand her question. For Samuel of course. Isn't it?

"You will think about this, yes?"

That's it?

She squeezes my hand. "Good. Now for your friend. I know some people who can perhaps help."

"Thank you."

Freda reaches over and puts her hand over mine. "Trust me, Lauren. Like me, you will survive this."

That night I dream of babies. Hundreds of them, crying in filthy cots. So many souls unloved. I miss Harry. I miss my mum. I wonder what life would be like if she never got sick.

It's déjà vu, back in the Starlight Room. Nerves and all. Paul is a great pianist and seems a nice guy, but his rhythm is different. So is the resonance of his notes, the whole sense of his playing. I'm stiff and awkward, constantly smoothing my dress and adjusting the angle of my microphone. What would Harry say? "You can't please everyone. Just be yourself." But who am I? That's the question.

I try slowing my breath, using my diaphragm for support. I visualise my body relaxing, my neck muscles, my shoulders, my arms – a soft, warm cloud of love descending on me ... Nope. I focus on my voice, keeping my larynx low, my jaw loose. I concentrate on the lyrics, it's just me and the song. Let everything else disappear. Nada. Will I ever get this?

Thank god the first bracket is over. Paul buys me a vodka and soda, and we take our break.

"How's it going?" he asks.

"Good. You?"

"Yeah, okay. You've got a great voice. Do you mind me asking? You seem a little tense."

"Oh, shit. Is it that obvious?"

"No, no, you've got a great voice—"

"Well, I haven't performed that much. I thought Harry would have told you."

He makes a face, but I can't tell what he's thinking. Do I suck?

"You just need to loosen up a bit. That's all. Relax."

"Ha."

"What?"

"Harry tells me that all the time. I don't know what it is, but I can't seem to let go. And the gaps between the songs – I can't hide behind the music there, and I have no idea what to say."

"Patter. It's called patter. You'll get it. It comes with time. Just say something interesting about the next song, chat about something funny that happened to you today, ask if people are enjoying their meal, that kind of thing."

"It sounds so easy."

"Bit more experience, you'll get there."

He reaches into his jacket pocket, takes something out and fiddles under the table with it. He looks around to make sure no-one is watching, then pops a tablet in his mouth. I must look shocked because he says, "Panadol. Got a headache."

I keep staring. The guy's full of it. Why would he hide Panadol?

"What? You want one? Here, give me your hand."

He pulls my arm underneath the table, reaches into his jacket pocket, then places a small plastic packet in my hand. The tablet is pink. I try to lift my hand to look more closely, but he drags my arm down.

"Careful."

"What is it?"

"Just something to loosen you up."

"Am I that tight?"

I flush at my own innuendo. Paul smiles but refrains from going there. "You're okay. It'll just warm you up. Make you feel good."

I hesitate. Alcohol is my strongest drug. I've never even smoked dope. Why would I take something harder?

"Relax. It's just a Molly. It won't hurt you."

"Molly?" I flip the packet over in my hand. The tablet's got a smiley face on one side.

"E. Look, you don't have to take it. You can give it back. They're not cheap."

I close my hand around it. "How do you know it's safe?"

"I have a reliable source."

I laugh. A reliable drug dealer? Isn't that an oxymoron? Still, people do these all the time, don't they? I'm nervous, but it could be fun. "How long does it take?"

"Depends. Everyone's different. Could be fifteen minutes, sometimes an hour."

It's time to go back on. Paul heads up to the piano. The tablet is still in my hand, the packet becoming sticky with the heat and sweat of my palm. Yes or No?

What's the big deal? Paul looks fine. He says he feels great. It would be so good to step on stage and not feel tense, unworthy. I want confidence. I want to own that stage. I open the packet, shake the tablet into my hand and look at it. Harmless. Small. Pink. Do it. Just do it. I lift my hand. The E is in my mouth. I take a sip of my drink, swallow, but the pill is still there. It won't go down. What am I doing?

I cough it back into my hand, scrape it back into its packet and tuck it in my purse. My life is too out of control as it is. I settle for sculling my vodka. And several more, during the night.

15

Amelioration

Snap's sitting on the edge of his hospital bed complaining that I've brought him the wrong jacket. Apparently, I can't tell the difference between corduroy and velour.

"What's it matter when you're wearing PJs underneath?" I ask.

"Mmmatters... tooo meee."

Even though he's slurring, his tone still has a snotty arrogance to it. It's good to know the stroke hasn't affected his attitude, but I'm sure he'd be saying a hell of a lot more than "mmmatters" if he had a better grip on his facial muscles.

"Freeeda's gumming this aft... nooon," he says.

"Coming."

"Gumming."

"C ... C ... coming."

"C... coming."

He's getting much easier to decipher, though it's hard not to look away when his twisted mouth is trying to produce words. It's as if he's doing something awkward or embarrassing that should be done in private. And I've caught myself talking to him as if he's a child – slowing my words or speaking louder than necessary. He doesn't react, so I can't tell if he's annoyed or not. If it were me, I'd want to slap someone.

"Freda is coming in this afternoon?"

Snap nods and points to my iPad on his bedside drawer. I've lent it to him because his doctor suggested some apps for cognitive improvement and speech building. I put it on the bed next to him, and he taps out a message with his right hand: Thanks. Legal stuff complicated.

"You're welcome, but let's talk, not type. While I'm in here anyway."

He looks as if he's about to lose it at me. He knows. I know. He doesn't need reminding. His therapist tells him every day: the more he practises his speech – and limb use – the quicker he'll recover. The first months are crucial. I'm torn between giving tough love and being a shoulder to cry on. Snap thumps his chest and grunts.

"Hey!" I grab his arm and tough love wins. "Don't do that. I know it sucks, but this is how it is. For now. Your body is doing the best it can. Show it some love."

I give him a hug, but he's still not happy. I don't blame him. Apart from the speech thing, the prospect of having to rely on other people must suck. Especially for normal stuff you should be able to do yourself, like opening a bottle of water, or pulling up your undies. And people let you down. Even the ones who are supposed to care, like his grandmother.

I thought she might show up after our talk. Maybe she's embarrassed at not having been there for him when he was growing up? Afraid he'll reject her. She shouldn't be. Snap's not like that. He only blusters because he thinks she never cared. That she's like his dad. How do I get Snap and Shirley to connect? They need each other.

I'm glad I decided not to tell him about visiting her though. Even if it's kind of lying by omission – it's for his own good – just like Harry lied to me. Actually, just like Snap went behind my back, contacting Harry in the beginning. Now that I think about it, we're all as bad as each other. Still, it doesn't feel good to keep secrets, and it may not end well, but I'm taking Freda's advice and learning to trust my instincts.

Just to be sure I'm not misjudging the woman, I test the waters. "I don't suppose any of your family has been in touch?"

Snap shakes his head.

"No-one?"

"Fug them."

"C, c, Fu... ck them."

He laughs. "C, c, couldn't give a fug. Ffffffu... ck."

That answers that. What a loser his gran is. She has an amazing grandson here. Yeah. People. They let you down.

I bend to help him with some slippers I've picked up at Kmart – he's never owned a pair in his life, he tells me – and we head off at old man's pace towards the cafeteria. He leans on a cane with his right hand, his left arm dangling – though he does have some use of it: I've seen him exercise it in his daily therapy sessions. This morning's session must have tired him out. I've been tempted to point out how lucky he is that it's his left side affected, seeing as he's right-handed, but I suspect "lucky" isn't in his vocabulary at the moment.

I help him sit, then head to the counter.

"Va ... nilla sly," he calls.

I turn back. "Vanilla slice?"

He nods.

Soft. Okay – easy to chew with a wobbly mouth, I can understand that, but what's with his sudden obsession with sweet stuff? Biscuits, chocolates, lollies just aren't his style, yet he's been hoeing into them like a hog searching for truffles. Depression? A side effect of his stroke? I guess some changes are inevitable. Whatever. If it gives him solace, it's all good. I'll join him.

I return with our order on a tray, and I haven't even finished transferring the cups to the table when Snap picks up his slice and tries to bite it. It's like watching a toddler trying to navigate his first meal. Custard squidges between his fingers, and he dribbles from the slack side of his mouth. Caught up in a moment of revulsion, I'm suddenly ashamed. I put the tray aside and reach for the sugar dispenser, adding too much to my cup.

"Disgussing?" he asks.

I glance at my own slice and consider shoving it at my face to make a messy show of solidarity. It might make us laugh. But then I wonder if he'd think I was sending the message he looks like a pig. I'd kill for a degree in psychology right now. "No. You look like you're enjoying it." I point to my own face. "You've got some custard here on your left cheek."

He wipes the opposite side to where I'm pointing, and I redirect him, wondering if his brain has reversed his perception or whether he can't process what I'm showing him. No, I've done that myself before. "Your other left."

"Would you like me to cut it up for you?" I ask. Is that going too far?

He drops the slice and looks at it for a moment, then nods. I ask the woman behind the café counter for a knife. She hands over a plastic one. I cut up my own slice while I'm at it. It's the least I can do to help him feel normal.

"So, another week or so, and they give you a Get Out of Jail Free card?"

Snap brightens. "Nnnot sooon nuff."

"The nurse said we can get council assistance. Someone to call in once a day, take you to rehab, help with cooking, cleaning, showering. All that stuff."

The noise he makes is almost a growl. "Don't need loook... ing after," he says.

"You want me to move back in? Maybe I should. Harry won't mind. I can check on his apartment every other day."

He shakes his head.

"Don't be a dick then. Accept the help. Hell, I'd kill for someone to cook and clean."

He looks morose.

"You know I'll come by most days too, see if you need anything personal."

"Don't neeed yooou either."

God, I imagine this must be what it's like planning an elderly relative's move to a retirement centre. That thought makes me twinge, because of Mum. But here's Snap, and going by his face, this is more like his last rites. He pushes his plate away.

"Don't be like that. I'm trying to help you." His eyes are shiny with tears, and it breaks my heart. "I'm sorry. But we have to talk about these things. It's not forever – it'll get better in time. Especially because you're young. You've got your whole..." I stop before I get the platitude out.

He shrugs.

"Can I organise some of your friends to visit? Keep you company?"

"No."

"Alright then."

I leave it for now. I'll ask again when he's in a better mood. At some point we'll have to talk about signing some sort of documentation so I can do banking and stuff for him – for the "just in case" he refuses to talk about. Maybe Freda can give us some guidance.

"Any hot male nurses in your rehab sessions?"

At last, I get a smile.

16

Inauspicious

The jangling noise jolts both me and Mr Pink. He chirrups and thumps to the floor. I flounder, wondering where the hell I am until I realise I didn't make it to bed last night – I'm sprawled on the couch. The television is on. The jangling is still going. It can't be the phone. It doesn't sound like that. I dig around and find my mobile on the floor. Crap. It's an alarm. My audition is this afternoon. I've got an hour to get my act together.

I jump in the shower with my forehead throbbing as though a bass player has crashed a party in my skull and is refusing to be told it's closing time. I did it to myself. I don't deny it. Another gig with Paul and too much vodka. Maybe I shouldn't have said no to the E. "Miniature passports to a temporary heaven," Paul said. "No hangover." Maybe I should have listened to him.

Harry's going to kill me. Well, at least I actually made the call and got an audition slot. Thank god I didn't leave learning the song until the last minute. I'll just go over it in the car a few times on the way there. My stomach grumbles. How long is it since I've eaten? I try to sing some scales while

I'm in the steam of the shower. Argh, my throat is sore. I cough and phlegm rattles in my chest. Great timing.

I'm puffing by the time I reach the theatre. The heavy glass door swishes closed behind me, and the sound of the city disappears. The foyer is all marble floors, columns, chandeliers and high ceilings.

"Sorry I'm late."

A girl wearing a Les Mis t-shirt over her jeans leads me through a side door. It opens to a corridor of chipped walls and aged linoleum. About fifteen hopefuls are sitting in chairs that line each side of the hallway.

"Take a seat," t-shirt girl says cheerfully. She hands me a clipboard with a form and pen. "Fill this out. Wait for your name to be called. Shouldn't be long."

I guess long is a matter of interpretation. An hour might not be lengthy in the real world, but in my hungover world it's an age. It's also the difference between getting to my afternoon shift at the store and getting the sack.

I try to swallow away the achy thickness in my throat, hoping the lozenge I'm sucking will work a miracle. I glance at the other applicants. A couple are chatting like good friends. Another is looking at the ceiling, humming scales. Others are staring at the wall, lost in thought or relaxed in daydreams. They look so confident.

A new arrival sits next to me. She looks fortyish, her generous body stuffed into a tight-fitting dress, and she doesn't seem to give a fig. Her nose is crooked, but her smile is big, warm and coated in hot pink lipstick.

"Newbie?" she asks.

I nod.

"I'm Beth," she says, offering her hand.

I shake it. "Lauren."

"You're looking a little under the weather there, darl."

"Yup."

"Nervous?"

"Yup."

"Don't be. They're humans just like you and me."

"You know them?"

"Oh, darls. I've probably slept with most of them." Her laugh is raucous, and I can't help but smile. "Only joshin". This'll be my tenth show with this company. Started in my early twenties. Once it's in your blood, there's no going back. Where's your music?"

"Oh, crap. I forgot it. Can't I just sing without it?"

She smiles. "What are you singing?"

"Umm, "I Dreamed a Dream"."

Beth nods. "Tell you what. If you get called in first, you can borrow my libretto." She holds up a whole book of music.

A door opens, someone exits, and the next victim is called. The process continues with the same routine: muffled talking for a couple of minutes, the piano starts up, then singing. So far two people have sung my song. A third is singing it now, and she sounds really good. There's more muffled talking, then the door opens. The girl's face is blank as she leaves.

Finally, the guy at the door calls my name. God, are they going to want to hear that song again? I hope they don't ask me to sing something else because it's the only one I've learned.

Beth hands me her libretto. "Here you go, darl."

I jerk to my feet like a school kid reporting for roll call. My coat falls to the floor. The guy sitting next to me picks it up.

"Thanks."

"Chookas," Beth calls.

Chookas? What the hell is that? "You too," I say, just in case it's some weird blessing.

Inside, the room is cavernous and musty. There's a woman and two men sitting at a trestle table. The door guy takes my clipboard and music, then tells me to stand a few metres in front of the trestle table where there's a bit of black tape on the floor. X marks the spot. There's no microphone. How is my voice going to carry?

For a moment, I stare at the tape, wondering whether to stand in front or behind it. I look up, and it's like I'm on The Voice, and these are my judges.

"So, Lauren, you'd like to audition for the role of Fantine?"

I nod mutely. Why am I here? I'm kidding myself.

"Okay. It's says here you're currently singing in lounges, bars, that sort of thing? Any musical theatre experience?"

I shake my head.

"Lauren, if you're going to be on stage, you're going to have to speak at some point. We need to hear your voice."

"Yes," I blurt. "I'm a singer."

They laugh. I cringe. Idiot.

"Okay, Lauren. Let Carol know when you're ready."

"Okay. Umm, just to warn you, I'm getting a cold ... so my voice isn't that—"

"Just do your best."

I turn to look at the pianist. To her credit, her expression doesn't say "not another Fantine wannabe". She smiles. I try to smile back. Please get me out of here. The intro starts. I suck in the biggest breath, nearly cough up my lungs, then try again at a gentler pace.

My left leg is shaking, and a nerve in my cheek twitches. I'm sure my first note is flat, but I push through, getting stronger with each line. It sounds okay; my voice is clear and reverberates off the walls. I'm getting it down, word for word, when suddenly there's a sharp, dry patch in my throat that catches. No matter how much I swallow, it won't go away. I cough and try to sing again but end up coughing more.

The two guys are murmuring to each other. The woman is looking at her notes. I have no idea what to do next. Carol comes over and hands me the sheet music. Her voice is gentle.

"Good job. Tough break, hey? There's a water fountain outside, if you need it."

"Thanks." I point to the door, still clearing my throat. "Do I go now?"

She smiles. "Just wait a moment, dear."

The panel are still chatting. I'm straining to hear but can't. I look around the room. The wooden floors are scuffed, portraits of people posed in costumes line the walls – people I should probably know, if I want to be in theatre – and an exit sign flickers over a fire escape at the far end. Ha. I should make a run for it.

"Lauren?"

"Yes?"

"That's all thank you. We'll let you know."

I arrive at work late and get yelled at. I'm on final notice.

I knew it. I should have waited another half-hour to have my shower, but I thought I could wing it. I've just rinsed the shampoo from my hair, and here's Harry calling. He always rings the landline around this time. He hasn't figured out how to dial my mobile from the ship's phone – too many pre-codes. He tried for three days in a row, but he kept getting some foreign-sounding dude who didn't speak a word of English but was really eager to chat. Harry said on the third attempt, the guy put his wife on the line, and she sounded pretty pissed off. I suggested it could have been two o'clock in the morning wherever they were.

So here I am, running down the hallway to the kitchen, wrapped in a towel, my hair dripping.

"Hi."

"Hello, you. You sound a bit snuffly."

The line is crackly, but hearing his voice is like a shot of chocolate to my veins, sweet and satisfying. "Yeah, got a cold. How's tricks?"

"Same, same. You?"

Mr Pink is winding himself between my feet, leaving bits of fur on my ankles. I slip onto a kitchen stool and lift my feet onto the rungs. "Well, I've got some good news and some bad news."

"Let's hear the bad first."

"I did that audition."

"And?"

"Don't ask."

Harry is silent for a moment. "Come on. Couldn't be that bad."

I screw up my face at the memory of my humiliation. "Yeah, it was. I stuffed up. Big time. You know what? I don't think theatre's for me. They were nice and all, but they don't even have microphones. And I was so freakin' nervous. I'd rather just work with you."

Harry laughs.

Mr Pink is licking water off the top of my foot. His tongue is scratchy. "Get off." I shoo him away.

"What?"

"Not you. The cat."

"Ah. Okay. Sorry to hear that. But I'm sure it wasn't that bad. You always underestimate yourself. It's part of your charm."

"Yeah, right." Still, I smile because it's him.

We chat about Snap for a while, then he says, "So, anyway, I've got some news that'll hopefully make you feel better."

There's excitement in his voice. I perk up. "What?"

"How do you feel about joining me for two weeks? Around twelve days actually."

"Serious?"

"Yep."

He tells me Tash, the girl he's been working with, can't handle the sea. "I kept telling her to take Travacalm, but she's one of those hippy types, you know, ginger tablets, herbal tea. It ended up costing her a couple of hundred bucks for a nausea injection last night. She was first off the ship this morning. Flying home from Noumea. I'm working solo the rest of this leg."

"You're really talking me into this glamorous South Pacific life," I say, picturing myself hanging over a rail, spewing my heart out. I've never been in a dinghy let alone a massive cruise ship.

Harry picks up on my doubt. "You'll be fine. Besides, only one way to find out. There's still twelve days left on this leg. See if you can get yourself well and get a fast-tracked passport."

"Wow. Okay. I'll see what I can do."

"Oh, one more thing," he adds. "Do you feel comfortable sharing a cabin with me? I'm sharing with a couple of other guys at the moment and Tash was sharing with another girl. We can do that too, or we can get our own cabin. Bunk beds. Up to you. No pressure."

"With you," I answer without thinking too much. A stranger doesn't appeal.

"Cool."

He fills me in on all the basics I'll need, and I make a quick list. "And don't forget the Travacalm. And some earplugs if you want any sleep," he finishes.

"You better keep a barf bag ready, just in case."

He laughs. "Miss you."

I smile. Those two words are like a hug. "Me too."

I hang up feeling as if I've just won something amazing for nothing. Twelve days in the South Pacific. Oh shit, I'm going to have to quit the convenience store. No way will my boss give me the time off. Tough. I was thinking of quitting anyway.

I sit and recount the conversation, to commit this moment to memory, see if I missed anything important. Sharing a cabin? I've been keeping so busy I haven't let myself think about our last encounter. Deep breath. Don't go there. I'll have my own bunk, my own space to retreat to. It'll be fine. Think of something else.

And it occurs to me that I forgot to tell Harry the good news: Snap is coming home early.

17

Impasse

Snap drops his keys for the second time. "Shooot!"

I'm impressed by how much his diction has improved the last couple of weeks. If he didn't get stuck on his vowels, he'd be rocking it.

He bends to retrieve his keys, then bites his lip in concentration as he tries to feed the key into the lock again. I retrieve a tissue and wipe my tender red nose. This would all be a hell of a lot easier if he'd just use his right hand, but he won't. "Rehab says the more I uuuse left side, the better." I keep my mouth shut, fighting the instinct to help him. Let him be. If determination alone will get that door open, Snap will succeed.

Finally, the lock turns, and he pushes the door open. I bend to grab his carry case, but he whacks the back of my head.

"Stop baaaybeeeing meee."

"Fine! You do it." I step back, more miffed at myself than him. Leave him be.

I'm glad I prepared the apartment before I brought him home — a good spring clean, the blinds are all up, there's autumn sunshine. Even the little pot plant I bought for the kitchen bench has managed to hang onto its tiny white buds. They're unfurling now, reminding me of the buds on his gran's magnolia tree. Beginnings. At least I thought they were.

"Niiice," Snap says, leaning his cane against the bench and taking a few stiff steps on his own, his left leg still a bit draggy. "I get it," he says. "Impatiens. Impatient patient."

"Sure," I say, wishing I really had thought of that. "I've scheduled some of your friends to drop by every couple of days. There's a list on the bench so you know who's coming when."

I wait for his usual grumble about how he doesn't want people fussing over him, but he surprises me. "Ta." He eases himself onto the couch and checks out his Zen garden. He may not have full control of his features, but I know a look of disgust when I see one.

I grimace. "Yeah, sorry about that. I did my best." I sneeze. "Sorry about that too."

He leans forward and grasps the tiny rake with his good hand, sifting the sand to his liking. I sit opposite him, and a flashback of him slumping in his chair, his tea spilling in his lap, hits me. He sees my face, and his expression softens.

"S'okaaay." The right side of his face is tense as he concentrates, the left looks saggy, like his brow might slide down and puddle onto his chin. "Yooou don't have tooo staaay. Go home. Rest."

It's excruciating waiting for him to get his vowels out. I swing my legs over the arm of my easy chair, trying to look as if I'm settling in. "Don't be silly. I've got nowhere to be a few hours. I'm on late shift."

He shrugs. "Teee?"

"Sure." I swing my legs back, ready to get up, but he waves me off.

"Sit." He pushes himself off the couch. "Soooner I show I'm okaaay, soooner I get rid of yooou."

"A girl never felt so welcome."

"Poor pet. Can't blaaame meee for missing your cruuuise this time."

I twist to look over the back of my chair. "Is that what you think? That I blame you?"

He stops halfway to the kitchen bench. "Just saaaying I can manage. Yooou gotta dooo your own thing now. No excuuuses."

I'm floored. I'd never thought of him lying unconscious in a hospital bed as an excuse. Does he mean I was looking for a way to get out of the cruise with Harry? No way. I wanted to go. But who else was going to stay by his side? His sometimes-friends? I watch his face, trying to determine if he's just being tetchy.

"Don't worry. I'm definitely going this time. Whether you cark it or not. Five days and I'm outta here."

He laughs. "That's myyyy girl."

But the thought won't leave me alone. Is he saying I chickened out? I think I've been freakin' brave. I haven't fallen apart. Much. No, look at him. He must be scared. It's huge coming home again.

Outside, beyond the glass door, dead leaves are scattered on the balcony. I should have swept those up. I look around the lounge for anything else I might have missed. The blank television screen is dusty. I shiver. The room feels lifeless, as if the energy was sucked out when they took Snap out on the stretcher, as if our apartment's personality has to start all over again along with Snap's poor body. I wish he'd come with me to Harry's. Just for a few days. But he won't. He wants to find his feet on his own. He doesn't even want me here.

I watch him in the kitchen, on the other side of the island bench, and I ponder how long it will take me to reach him if he drops the steaming kettle on himself, or smashes a cup, or slips over.

He catches my eye and pauses to shake his head. "Don't dooo that."

"What?"

"Pity. I can feeel it from heeer."

"Oh, please. As if." I try to think of a smart-arse response, but it won't come.

"Yooou can dooo better than that," he drawls. "I can handle it."

He's wrong; I can't.

He motions to me. "Okaaay, come get. I'm not careee-ying both."

"Now you're being obtuse." I go over to him and lean across the counter. When I reach for both cups, he smacks me.

"Taaake your own."

"Ow." I rub my hand. "That freakin' hurt."

He smirks. "Ha. Yooou should seee your faaace. Loooks like a gat's bum."

"Cat. C... c... cat. Yeah, well it's not as bad as your face." I stare at him, horrified at my words.

Half his face grins while the rest slumps. It's awful to look at. "Not as bad as yooou in your stinky convenience store clothes," he says.

"Not as bad as you when you're pretending to orgasm on your phone sex line."

He cracks up. "Not as bad as yooou the morning after a gig."

I laugh. "Yeah, well, shit happens. I can't always be bothered taking make-up off at that time of the morning."

He joins me back in the lounge room. "Yooou don't neeed make-up, honey. You're beeeuuutiful," he says.

"Not as beautiful as your friend in rehab. I saw him through the window at your last session." Snap blushes. I've hit gold, so I sing-song to him, "Someone's got a crush. Someone's got a crush. What's his name?"

Snap's blush deepens, and he refuses to meet my eyes.

"O.M.G. Is this true love?"

"B..." he stumbles.

"Bertie? Bernard? Barnaby? Beetlejuice? Bazza?"

"B... B..."

"Spit it out."

He laughs, his shoulders shaking with the effort. "Bitch."

"Ha. That's why you love me."

"Ben."

"The Flower Pot Men!"

"Well, heee's definitely a panseeey if he likes meee."

"I'm happy for you."

Snap smiles into his cup as he sips. The blush suits him: it gives him a look of health that's been missing for weeks. I'm really am happy for him.

He asks how Harry is.

"He's fine. Enjoying the cruise."

Snap seems satisfied with my answer. We both settle into quiet, staring at his Zen garden. It looks perfect. Every pebble and grain of sand where it should be. Don't breathe.

I sneeze.

Snap looks as if he's found nirvana in one of Freda's burgers. He stops between bites to mop up stray sauce dribbling from his bun, not wanting to waste a drop. I guess weeks of hospital food has piqued his appetite for some truly tasty indulgence.

I've settled for a large orange juice; my throat's still raw. This bug looks as if it's here for the long haul. Not surprising. It's been the longest week of my life. I never knew I could cram so much into seven days – my job shifts, the audition, gigs, arranging my passport, bringing Snap home, helping him get settled with daily home help from the council – thank god he's relented – researching disability allowances, grocery deliveries, and sorting out our share of rent and bills. There's probably loads of other stuff neither of us has considered. At least we've worked our way through all the leaflets the hospital gave us.

And hooray for my passport arriving in perfect time to join Harry. Three more days, and I'll be out of here – sick or not.

Snap scoots over as Freda approaches us. She's got some news for us on Snap's case, but her face is giving nothing away. My stomach is tight with worry. I'm sure she would have told us straight away if it was good news. Instead she insisted we eat first.

"I have spoken with my lawyer friend. He says it might be difficult to prove this violence was a direct cause of your stroke. He says they might claim there could have been a pre-existing condition. In this case, you cannot win. It's a risk."

For a moment, I'm thrown by her bluntness. Then I can't help myself. "This is bullshit!" I'm not pissed because of what she's telling us, but because she's confirmed what I already suspected through my Google searches. One major case I saw on YouTube should have been clear-cut: three bouncers knocking down a guy and restraining him – one by lying on top of him. The guy couldn't breathe. He had a heart attack. He died. But the court case verdict? Not guilty. Why? The guy had a prior heart condition. But that's not Snap. Snap is young. He's healthy, was healthy, he's fit, he takes care of himself.

Snap grasps my arm across the table. "Shhh."

Freda nods, looking like a sage beyond her thirty-odd years. An owl. That's how I'd describe her. Big eyes that carry wisdom handed down from generations. But I don't want wisdom. I want justice.

"You can take this Bob to court, but this is risky. You might receive some compensation, or you might lose and have to pay costs."

I know Freda is doing us a favour here, but my hands are tight fists. I want to smash someone. "It's not fair. It's so not fair!"

"Fuck." Snap drops his head onto his arms.

My heart is crushed for him. How did this happen? It all seemed so clear-cut a moment ago. Bob did this. We all know it. Now he's going to get away with it.

Freda taps Snap's arm. I don't like the dourness of her face. "Snap, I think you have something to say about this. Yes?"

Snap raises his head and drags his hand over his face, elongating the good side to match the droopy one. He shakes his head slowly as if he's trying to loosen a nightmare that won't leave. "Mmm ... my father."

Freda is relentless. "Something else?"

"No." He turns to me. "Let's go."

We stop at a red light, and the indicator's tick tick tick is like a bomb counting down. I take my hands off the wheel and stretch my fingers. They're cramping from gripping the steering wheel so tightly. Snap is staring out the passenger window, jaw set. The lights change, and I drive forward.

"You okay?" I ask. I glance at him when he doesn't answer. "Snap?" Still no answer. "What did you mean about your dad? Do you think he has something to do with your stroke? His beatings maybe?"

In my peripheral vision, he's shaking his head. "Then what?"

"Can't yooou put it tooogether?"

"Humour me."

He sighs. "Why do yooou think he's in a wheeelchair?"

"You told me he had an accident."

"I lied."

"What? Snap ..." I venture guilty, harbourer of my own secrets, "don't you trust me?"

He folds his arms, angry, or defensive. Maybe both. "It's not about yooou."

I purse my lips. "So ... what's the real story?"

Snap slaps his head. Then again. And again.

"Stop it. What are you doing?"

"It's our brains! There's something wrong with our brains."

"Snap!" I try to grab his hand while trying to steer. He's hyperventilating.

"Are you saying he had a stroke too?"

"I didn't want tooo feel guilty about leeeaving him alone," he says.

"No, Snap. No. You shouldn't feel guilty. Else I should too. I haven't exactly been the perfect daughter myself; Mum is still languishing in the hospice. But she has people looking after her, and your dad would have his church people, wouldn't he? He's not alone at all. And besides, he's an arsehole. He doesn't deserve you."

"Doesn't mmm ... make it feeel any less bad."

He slaps himself again.

"Don't do that. You're not bad."

"Fff ... forget it. It's nnn ... not worth it."

"But you can still try to press charges against Bob, get some victim compensation."

"No."

"You can't let him get away with this, Snap." As soon as I say the words, I realise what a double-edged sword they are. He doesn't bother coming back at me. He knows.

I swear as I narrowly miss a pothole. Finally, we turn the corner and pull up at our apartment. I squeeze the steering wheel, unsure of what to do with my anxiety.

There's an idea going through my head, one I wish would go away, because it makes me sick to think I might be his only chance ... because going to court would be ... I've heard too many horror stories about dragging up a victim's history when it comes to sex-related crimes. But if I'm really Snap's friend, I should to do it. It's the right thing to do.

I steel myself. "If you press charges ... I will too."

Snap is motionless. I wonder if he's heard me. I touch his arm. "Snap?"

He shrugs me off, still staring out his window. Does he have any idea what it took for me to say that? How terrified I am? No, you idiot, I remind myself. How could he? I've never told him about Samuel. How that hate is buried so deep. How I'd do anything not to let it surface in case it consumes me. Breaks me.

I watch his profile, his furrowed forehead, the tenseness in his jaw. In the fading light, his right side looks perfectly normal, now that his hair has grown over the scar. He's like the beautiful Snap I used to know. He's still beautiful, I remind myself. He's still Snap. But what's going on in that head of his?

I wait, giving him some time to gather his thoughts. A bee lands on the windscreen. I watch its fuzzy body crawl along the wiper, and I try to remember how long bees live for. Is it weeks or months? Imagine that: living your short life to serve. No ego. No other higher purpose. Nothing hidden. No secrets. No lies.

I touch Snap's arm. Speak gently. "Are you okay?" He's a stone. "Do you want me to stay? I don't have to go. I can stay. Harry will understand."

I don't think Harry will understand, but I'm worried. What if Snap does something awful? "Come on," I say, pulling the keys from the ignition. "Let's go inside. It's vodka o'clock. We'll do some shots, take stock, makes some plans. At least we know where we stand now."

"We?"

I'm stung by his sarcastic tone. It was shitty news today, but he doesn't need to take it out on me. I try to deflect his mood. "Yes. We. We're in this together. Let's chill tonight, order up a pizza, get drunk and forget about this crap for a while."

Snap makes a strange, strangled noise and pushes his door open. He stumbles onto the nature strip, then starts up the driveway. I grab my bag, jump out and follow.

"Wait up."

I follow as he heads towards the apartments. Anger must be an effective cure because he's walking like there's nothing wrong with him. No drag, no limp. It's definitely a stalk. He reaches the stairs and uses his good arm to hoist himself, quickening his pace. When he gets to his front door, he turns on me, face contorted and red.

"Piss off. I don't need you."

His words are a slap. I reel back. When I respond, I'm all breathy and squeaky. "How dare you!"

"How dare?" White spots of anger speckle the redness of his cheeks. "Look at you, all goody two shoes. Ready to sacrifice yourself for me."

"What? I'm trying to help you."

"I don't need your help."

"I can't believe you. I've stayed by your side this whole time. I bent over backwards to help. I gave up my cruise. I... I've put my life on hold for you."

"Who asked you to? Did I ask you to?"

"No. You didn't need to. It's what friends ..." I'm floored. What an ungrateful... pig! And the fact that he got all those words out without even a stumble, tells me how much effort he's putting into hurting me. He stares as though he doesn't even recognise me, and I wonder if he's having another stroke, or if we're going to have a bitch fight, right here on the landing, for all the neighbours to hear.

"God!" I spit back. "I didn't ask you to defend me against Bob either. Look where that got you."

"Oh, fuck off."

"You fuck off."

It's then he crumbles. He falls back against the door and slides to the ground. His hands cover his face and his shoulders shake. It's the first time I've ever seen him cry. Ever. It kills me. I want to hug him, but I'm afraid to touch.

"Oh hun, we're both worn out. Let's go inside, get warm and calm down."

"I want tooo beee alone." He gets up, pulls his keys from his pocket and unlocks the door.

"Please, Snap," I persist, rubbing his arm.

He flicks me off. "I said no. You have no idea. You just don't know."

"What? What don't I know?"

He turns on me. "It was me! I threw the first punch. I hit him first." He's got the door open. He stumbles inside, then turns to block my entry. "There's no point. Just go away."

He shoves the door closed so hard, it's as if he's slamming out our friendship. I want to smash it down, insist that I stay. He shouldn't be alone. Not like this. But ... have I been too much in his face? Maybe alone time is all he needs. Time to calm down, think things through and cry where no-one can see his poor, distorted face.

Spent, I go downstairs and get back in the car. I sit for a while, then blow my nose, which has decided to start running – great, this bug is going to my head now – and try to absorb what just happened.

So where to from here? Do I leave his car here? He can't drive it. But it doesn't feel right to take it, since I'll be leaving soon for the cruise.

A splatter of white and brown hits the windscreen. I peer forward and up to the tree harbouring the offender. Why is it always when you're down? Screw it. I can use Harry's car if I need to. I get out and stand on the curb while I order an Uber on my phone. I text Snap:

Keys are in the letterbox.

I'm tempted to add "arsehole", but I love him too much.

18

Capitulation

I don't know if I'm going to make it through this last gig. The doctor said my bug is viral, no point taking antibiotics. I've had every chemist medicine known to man, but my throat still feels as if it's been left out to bake for three days in a desert, and my head is so thick with gunk I don't know if there's room for my brain.

Thank god I've got a stool to sit on, even though apparently management frowns on it – something about giving a "less dynamic" performance. It's either this, or I drape myself on the grand piano in an attempt to look sexy on a shiny, musical sick bed. Paul, bless him, has tried to find a last-minute fill-in but no luck. So here I am, a snotty pile of crap.

He offers me another E. "Supposed to be a good cough suppressant," he says. "It'll make you feel better, at any rate."

I haven't told him the first one he gave me is still sitting in my purse. I don't know why I've kept it. Probably because he says they're expensive. Or because some niggly part of me thinks maybe, one day ... if things get really tough.

"Thanks, but I'm okay."

He buys me a brandy, asking the bartender to add a dollop of honey and some hot water. I take tiny sips to make it last, mindful of only having one drink, since I to drove Harry's car here – the weather is so miserable tonight a tram was out of the question. That, and I need to cut back the alcohol before I hit the cruise.

Somehow, I scrape through, then head home to find some selfish dick has taken Harry's car spot. I reverse out and park by the curb. The flimsy evening wrap I'm wearing provides little protection against the damp night air, and I shiver as I hurry into the foyer. I was stupid to think driving meant I didn't need to rug up, because now I'm freezing my butt off, waiting for the ponderously slow lift. I comfort myself by thinking about seeing Harry on Friday. Two more sleeps. That's if they let me on the ship with this head cold. Harry's told me to not to mention it. OH&S stuff. But I feel bad. What if I pass it onto other passengers?

I console myself with imaginings of Harry's hugs making me forget my everyday crap, then grab a mussed-up tissue I've got tucked in my bra. The skin around my nose stings, red-raw from wiping it all night.

The landing light has blown, so I fossick through my handbag in the dark. "Damn it." Finally, I feel the metal tag in the bottom of my bag and pluck it out. I've been meaning to secure it to my own key ring ever since Harry gave it to me. I just haven't got around to it. Maybe it was an unconscious reflection of our relationship – tentative?

My frigid hands shake as I try several times to fit the key in the lock. The dark isn't helping. "Oh, come on. Just get in there, will you?" The key slips from my hand, hitting the ground with a metallic chink. The sound reverberates through the empty landing as does my "Fuuuck!" I lean my back against the door and slide down onto the concrete sill.

Immediately, I'm reminded of Snap, and I feel small. Trite. Am I doing the right thing leaving him on his own? What if he's depressed? What if he tries something... something I don't want to think about? Geez, it's been three days, Snap. Just answer my freakin' calls already. Let me know you're alright. If he doesn't answer by tomorrow, I'm going to stomp right over there and check on him in person. He's probably curled up on the couch, unwashed, unshaven and not eating. I wonder if he's letting the council staff in to clean.

Eventually the coldness of the concrete stirs me to action. I kneel forward feeling about for the key. There's the sucker.

While I wait for the kettle to boil, I lean against the sink, head tilted back, trying to relieve the pressure in my sinuses. It doesn't help. I'm due for some more Codral.

The kettle rumbles and clicks off, and I mix my drink, then sip as I look at my refection in the kitchen window. "You've come a long way, baby." Not far enough, an inner voice tells me.

Mr Pink wanders in with a chirrup. I squat beside him and give him a pat. "What do you think? Huh? I'm afraid you gotta rely on your owner for a couple of weeks, matey. I'll miss you though."

I turn off the lights and head for my bedroom. As I reach the doorway, I glance down the hallway towards Harry's room. I wander towards it. Several times over the past days I've climbed onto his bed and just lain there, trying to breathe in his fading scent. Pointless now with my blocked sinuses. I'll change his bedding for him before I leave, surprise him with fresh, clean sheets for when we get back.

For now, I don't want to lose what little essence of him remains. However fragile it is. Tonight, I'll sleep there and try to imagine we're in love. And that my body won't betray me.

That's it. I've had enough of Snap's silence. It's just plain rude. If my mobile phone was a landline receiver, I'd slam it. Instead, I tap the off button on the screen. Hard. As if it makes a difference. Damn him. I'm going to have to go over there. I can't stand not knowing if he's okay. I need to hear his voice. Not that I know what I'm going to do if he's not okay, because I'm leaving for my cruise tomorrow. Still, I have to know.

Okay, I'm going to try his mobile one more time. Maybe he was on the loo. I dial. The ringing tone is relentless, like a toothache that won't go away. Damn it. I try the landline. It's off the hook. Arsehole. If he thinks he can ignore me because he's in a foul mood, he better think again. Here I come. With my own key. I'm out the door. I'm in the car.

There's an inevitable bright flash at the intersection as I try to beat the red light. Freaking fantastic. Sorry, Harry. Calm, I tell myself. I've got to chill. It's my head cold making me cranky. I should be in bed, resting, trying to get rid of it before I leave. Fat chance. Shhh. Calm, remember? My foot doesn't listen and stays planted on the pedal.

When I get to Snap's I slam the car door, trying to use up some of my frustration-borne pissyness. It kinda works. As if I'm really going to yell at him anyway. Should I use my key and walk right in? No, it doesn't feel right. Stupid because I live here.

I knock, and there's barking and the sound of scrabbling of claws on the wooden floor inside. What the hell? Has he gone and got himself a dog? I tilt my head, considering the prospect and decide it's not a bad idea. Not bad at all. A furry friend to cheer him up. It's when the door opens that I get the biggest shock.

"Shirley!"

She stands there in a floral dress and blue cardigan, mini-George at her feet, staring at me. I must look like an idiot with my mouth open, wordless.

"Yes?" she says.

"Um, is Snap... George... home?"

"I'm sorry, George isn't seeing anyone right now. He's not well." She smiles, all sweet and light. "Aren't you the young lass who called in on me?"

"Yes. I'm Lauren."

"That's right. Look, I'd let you in, but he's only just fallen asleep."

I wonder if she realises she's stopping me from entering my own apartment. "Can I see him just for a minute? It's important."

"Oh love, he's got a shocking chest cold, been coughing all night. I'm sure you don't want to disturb him?" Her expression tells me it's not a question.

"Well ... I need to get a few things from my room too."

"Oh." She smacks her forehead. "I'm a stupid old cow. Sorry, sorry I forgot you live here."

She steps back and lets me through. "Please keep your voice down. I really don't want to wake him up."

"Sure. Thanks."

She follows me down the hall. I turn into my bedroom. What the hell? There's a suitcase on the floor, an unfamiliar coat on my chair, and the bed has been slept in.

Shirley whispers from behind. "I hope you don't mind. Snap said it would be okay if I stayed a few days. To look after him. If you need your room back ..."

My head is reasoning that it's a nice gesture, but this is my personal space she's invaded. Snap should have asked me first.

I try not to sound too pissy. "Sure. Why not?" I move to my wardrobe and look through my summer clothes for anything cruise-worthy. I might have to do some quick op-shopping.

Shirley is still hovering. "Can I make you some tea?"

"Coffee?" Anything for some privacy.

I gather a few personal bits and pieces — sunscreen, bathers, a beach towel, and look for something to throw them in. In the bottom of my cupboard, I find Snap's Hello Kitty backpack, the one I never returned because it was fun to banter over. I hope he's okay. Maybe I'll sneak a look in his room.

I push Snap's door open a fraction. The blind is drawn, and there's a vaporiser on the floor beside his bed, hissing eucalyptus steam. He's out cold, the doona pulled up to his chin, his hair pasted to his scalp. Poor thing.

In the kitchen, Shirley is waiting for the kettle to boil. There's a pile of chocolate chip biscuits on a plate. My stomach growls; I forgot breakfast.

"I'm sorry, but I don't know how to use this coffee machine." She points to the Aldi pod machine on the counter. The one Snap's always going on about replacing with a proper espresso machine with a gurgly milk frother. When we're rich.

"It's okay, I'll do it." I reach for the packet of pods, then think about the noise the machine is going to make. "Actually, I'll have tea too."

Shirley pops a bag in my cup. It's a different brand to our usual. She's either brought them with her or been shopping. She concentrates on negotiating the boiling kettle. I'm about to tell her to be careful, the lid's cracked, but she manages just fine with her shaky hands. Her fragility reminds me of Snap's first day out of hospital, when I forced myself to take a back seat and let him deal with everyday stuff.

Which makes me wonder: why has she only turned up now? Not when Snap really needed her? I'm blunt. "I thought you would have come to see him at the hospital."

She flinches, stops pouring and lowers the kettle to the bench. She looks thoughtful, choosing her words while focusing on the cups.

"I wanted to. I could have I suppose. But …" Her face is distressed, her hand moves to her forehead as if she has a sudden headache. I'm not sure if she's faking it.

"Hospitals remind me of all the time we spent … his mother …" She shakes her head. "And I thought he might be angry with me. Sending money is one thing but… I've missed so much time with my grandson." She smiles, hopeful. "He doesn't mind though. He's just happy I'm here now. And I'm happy to be here."

She waits for my response, as if seeking my approval. Or forgiveness. Something. I nod. She sighs. "I suppose I have you to thank for that."

I blush. Maybe she's real after all. "So, you're staying for a while?"

"I hope so. But … oh, if you need your room back—"

"No, no. I'm leaving tomorrow on a cruise. It's just Snap and I … well, he was kind of shitty with me when I last saw him. I wanted to make sure he was okay. I'm glad … relieved you're here to take care of him."

"Me too."

I chomp into a biscuit. "Starving."

"Good, hey? I made them," she says.

"Mmmm." I reach for a second one. I am glad she's here.

A few hours later, I've trawled the local op shops, scoring a couple of summer dresses, three t-shirts, a pair of cut-off shorts and old suitcase. As I arrive back home, my phone beeps.

Snap: *Soz Kitten. Phone on silent. Miss you. Forgive me? Know I've been a bitch. BTW Gran makes bitchin' scones. Come back tomorrow*

Me: *Can't. Cruise. See you in a couple of weeks. All forgiven. Love you.*

Snap:*!!!* ☐☐☐ *Go get him, girlfriend* ☐☐

19

Sanguine

I peer out the window as my taxi rolls into the terminal. Wide-eyed as a kid, I stare at the ship – a white giant, towering above the port buildings. Passengers huddle in a queue snaking towards the luggage dock. Most are rugged up against Sydney's drizzle, a few are hopeful in colourful summer clothing. They pull their wheeled suitcases behind, chatting and checking documents as they inch forward. I spot a young boy in a Hawaiian shirt, separated from his family. His face is tilted up, and he's frowning at what he probably imagined would be a humungous and pristine cruise liner. Humungous it is. Pristine it's not. Rust stains have dripped down its flanks, and as my taxi draws closer the layered patches where the rust has been painted over, again and again become apparent. Still, the ship's presence is impressive.

I spot Harry before he sees me. He's waiting outside the check-in terminal. I do a double take: he's shaved off his beard. I like it. Then I go all hot and flushy remembering being in his bed. Maybe he's forgotten? Fat chance; I was a fruitcake.

Now comes the crunch: how do we greet each other? I've been mulling over this dilemma on the plane trip, picturing him grabbing me, and me kicking up a heel, and us kissing like long lost lovers. Lame. Especially since I've still got this damned cold. But seriously. Do we hug? Exchange a peck on the cheek? Go back to our careful "professional" relationship? And then there's the cabin thing. Can I cope with that for twelve days?

Harry sees me and breaks into a grin. His teeth look ridiculously white against his tan. His hair is shorter, messy and wavy. Cute. He lopes towards the taxi, opening my door with a bow like a posh concierge. "Good trip, m'lady?" He tries to look bright-eyed for me, but he's obviously tired. Why? Aren't cruises supposed to be ... cruisey?

"Lovely, thank you. Have you prepared my cabin?"

"But, of course. How are you feeling?"

"Better. Still a bit snotty. Love the new look."

I pay the driver, then take Harry's offered hand. The wind catches my skirt as I climb out of the taxi. I focus on holding it down, glad for the distraction so I don't have to make the first move. Harry grabs me into a hug, then lets go. I deflate. No kiss? Still, what did I expect? I'm a walking germ factory.

"Look at that," he says, peering at the sky. "The rain just stopped."

I shrug, nonchalant. "Well, I did order clear weather for my arrival."

The driver pops the boot, and we head around the back of the taxi. Harry looks at the Hello Kitty backpack sitting beside my suitcase.

"Sweet."

I lift it up and tuck my purse into an outside zipper pocket. "No disrespecting the kitty bag. I kinda stole it from Snap."

Harry insists on carrying my suitcase. Fine by me. Inside the terminal, we queue for our passes, just like all the other passengers. I notice there's a separate line for crew that's moving quicker.

"Aren't we crew? Don't we get some perks?"

"No. We're guest entertainers. We get guest privileges. Trust me, it's better. Once we've done our gigs, we can do what we like. Crew have extra hours, extra duties."

The queue moves forward a place.

"You know, as soon as we get free time, and the sun decides to put in an appearance, you'll find me on a lounger, cocktail in hand."

Harry nods. "Have you brought some Travacalm?"

"Oh, yeah. I took it in the taxi. Not taking any chances."

Harry shuffles my suitcase forward as the line moves again. I turn my attention to the receptionist at the counter. Her hair is pulled back so tight it's giving her an eyebrow lift. She cheerfully greets each new passenger as they approach, then her expression drops as she doles out documents with a spiel she's obviously repeated a thousand times.

Harry pokes me in my side. "Excited?"

"Yeah." I crack a grin. I am. I actually am.

"Miss me?"

I look up, intending to give a flippant answer, but something in his eyes catches me off guard. I'm hit with the memory of him standing in the doorway of his apartment saying goodbye. He had the same look then. Uncertainty. And now something suddenly occurs to me: I have some power here.

"Nah." I toss my head, brushing off the moment.

"Me neither."

He nudges me with his shoulder, and I nudge him back. Good. Let's keep it light.

It takes a good forty minutes to reach the counter and another twenty in the luggage queue before we're free to board. We stop to have our photo taken at the security booth just inside the gangway. The booth operator is blank faced. I smile at him, but he doesn't respond.

"Passport and pass," he says. There's no "please".

We hand them over and Harry explains the process. "This is where we embark and disembark at islands with ports. Check-in, check-out. If there's no port, we take a tender. Same deal."

I assume a tender is some kind of boat, but I don't want to look stupid, so I nod. He leads the way along several corridors, then down two flights. A young, uniformed guy backs out of a cabin, pulling a vacuum cleaner with him. Harry's already told me most of the service crew are Filipino, and they live and work on the lower decks of the ship on six-month to year-long contracts. I can't imagine spending so much time with hardly any daylight.

"Thomas." Harry waves.

"Ah, Mr Harry. You're back for another trip?"

"Yep. I tried to escape, but they caught me." Harry turns to me. "Lauren, this is Thomas. He's the man to ask if you need something."

We shake hands, then Thomas moves aside so we can get by. We trundle further along the corridor and turn right. When we're out of earshot, I murmur, "Glad to see some of the crew are happy. That guy at the security booth could crack rocks with his face."

Harry nods. "Been on board too long. This rabbit warren can do your head in. Last week one of the orchestra musos got sacked for wandering around drunk in his underwear at two in the morning."

I snigger.

"It was funny until he got kicked off at the first island and had to pay his own airfare home to the States."

"Ouch."

"So, this is our room," Harry says, stopping outside a narrow cabin door. "I've moved my stuff in already. Nice to have a bit of privacy after sharing with two blokes." He puts the key in the lock, then turns to me. "I had to lie and say we were a couple to get this room. Doubles are in high demand."

Doubles? Does he mean double bed? Are we sleeping together? He never mentioned that before. I flick back through our previous conversations. Bunk beds. I'm sure he said bunk beds. All this time I've been wondering about how it would work sharing a bathroom, getting changed, getting into bed. Should I have brought PJs instead of my usual t-shirt and undies? I've been telling myself to just roll with it. It's only twelve days. If it gets awkward, it's not so long. And if it does work out, and things ... develop ... well, maybe we'll try crossing that bridge again if it happens. Baby steps. Stay calm, stay calm. Just wait. It might not be what you think.

Harry unlocks the door but turns to me again before he pushes it open. He grimaces apologetically. "Um, before you go in, there's one thing. There's something that needs fixing. And it will be fixed. I promise."

He steps back and lets me enter and, as I do, a gross stench takes my breath away, even though my nose is almost blocked. It's vomit-inducing.

"What is that?"

"Cigarettes. The musos before us were smokers."

"You're allowed to smoke down here? God, it smells like industrial chemicals."

"They're not supposed to. I think the sewerage lines must be backed-up a bit too. It'll clear once we leave port."

"God. It's like someone has left a basket of month-old stinky socks lying around."

"It's not as bad as the other room I've been sharing with two blokes."

I stare at him, disgusted. How can anyone live like this? There's no air. No window or porthole. Now I know where the term "bowels of the ship" comes from.

Harry leans against the doorway watching me. "I've asked for the room to be deodorised before we leave port. And we can keep the door open whenever we're in here."

"So much for the glamorous life."

I keep my hand over my nose and mouth as I take in the room and fittings. It's neat, clean – even if it smells like toxic chemicals have saturated the furnishings – and it's bigger than I expected. But it's only now I realise how distracted I've been by the smell, because the most obvious thing is single bunks. Crisis averted. Still, I'm surprised by a teeny-tiny bit of disappointment.

Harry pats the top bunk. "Mine."

"K."

"So ... you're okay with this?" he asks.

"Sure." I throw my backpack on the lower bunk. "I'm not great with heights."

"No, I meant with... everything."

"I'm not thrilled about the foul eau de cologne but if it gets fixed, it's okay."

I sit on my bunk and try to bounce. There's no spring, the bunk base is solid, and the mattress is half the thickness of my bed at home, but somehow, it's comfortable. There's a ledge against the wall to hold personal stuff and a little nightlight for reading.

"Afraid of heights, huh? You never told me that."

"Never came up."

"Guess we won't be doing that I'm the King of the World thing at the ship's bow."

Bolder, I give him a sly smile. "No, but maybe we can do other Titanic scenes."

"We can?"

Something in his eyes makes my pulse pick up. I didn't mean right now. Not in the starkness of a fluoro cabin light and with my head full of snot. I immediately stand up in case he thinks he's going to join me on my no-bounce mattress. He moves to the door and locks it. Oh shit. When he walks back to me, my brain is back-pedalling fast.

"You know what?" I say, "I'm a bit dry. Maybe we can get a drink or something?"

"Sure." He comes over, plants his hands on either side of my face, lowers his forehead to mine. Is this how bunny rabbits kiss? I like it. And if my nose wasn't half-blocked, and the room didn't stink so much, I'm sure I'd be able to smell his scent – earthy like his bed. And I'm sure it's not just my blocked nose that's making it difficult to breathe.

"Can I kiss you?" he asks.

I falter. The impulse to raise my face, to join my mouth to his, is overwhelming. "I'm phlegmy. You don't want you to catch anything," I murmur.

"I've got a good immune system."

He lifts my chin, lowers his mouth. A soft pressing of lips. I'm conscious of how tight I'm holding my mouth – hesitant, waiting to see if my body will betray me again. So far so good – maybe it's the thought of all the little cold germs running around in my saliva that's keeping the panic at bay. I put my hands on his shoulders, move closer. A tremor of warmth surges through me as his arms circle my waist, and he pulls me closer. I loosen my mouth. I want this, I really do, if my body will only co-operate.

Harry pushes me back towards the bunk. The top rack is lower than either of us anticipates, and I whack my head on the metal frame.

"Oww. Fufffffruit!"

"Geez, sorry. Are you okay?"

"No!" I sit on the lower bunk and rub my head.

Harry tries to smother a laugh. "Fuff-fruit?"

"Don't push it. I'm making an effort with the language. And it's not funny. It hurts."

"Let me see." He sits next to me and prises my hand off my head.

I huff. "Spell concussion. I think my skull is cracked."

"No blood. You're okay. Maybe we should save the reunion for later."

"You don't say."

There's one of those awkward silences while I lick my wounds. Harry deflects the conversation. "Tour?"

"Sure, but I hope they have a doctor on board if you're intent on killing me."

"Come here." He grabs me and gives the back of my head a rub.

"Ow." I shake him off. "Okay, let's go," I say, determined not to let a headache ruin my arrival. "Wait, what about my suitcase?"

"We'll get it later. Let's go. I'll show you where we'll be playing."

He takes my hand as we leave the cabin, and I'm surprised to feel him shaking a little. He's rattled. Something strange blooms in me again. Am I responsible for his happiness?

We pass through the narrow corridor and almost bump into one of our neighbours. Harry introduces me to Dwayne, a huge African American dude from New York.

The trombone player has a big belly and a deep laugh to match it. I take to him immediately.

"I'm lookin' forward ta hearin' ya missus sing," he says, his voice gravelly and chocolaty.

Missus? I flick a look at Harry, but he doesn't correct Dwayne. Instead he launches into telling him how he's found a copy of some jazz record in a pile of vinyls at a street stall in Noumea. I've never heard of the album, so I stick to mulling over the thought of being called a "missus". His missus. I guess if word gets around we're married, it might save me from being hit on.

We climb a couple of flights of stairs and enter the main lobby. It's wide and spacious with a grand central staircase. Several decks are visible above us, and guests are peering over the balustrades as though it's a viewing platform. There's a plaque on a nearby wall that says the ship is five times the size of the Titanic.

"Wow. That puts things in perspective," I say.

Harry shows me one of the lounges we'll be performing in. It's decked out in a safari-style theme, complete with a life-sized bronze tiger. I sit on it, side-saddle, while he takes a photo with his phone. Nervous excitement is bubbling up. This is real. This is happening. I'm a legitimate entertainer.

We leave the lounge and wander further down the ship to a set of lifts. As Harry presses the button for level twelve where the main restaurant is, I do a double take. The buttons skip from twelve to fourteen.

"Seriously? No thirteen? They actually do that?"

Harry looks at the buttons. "Ha. I never noticed."

"So the Sun Deck is really thirteen?"

"It's fourteen."

I give him a do-you-think-I'm-an-idiot look.

He wrinkles his nose. "We're playing up there for sail-away in a couple of hours."

"Let's hope thirteen is lucky for us."

Turns out it's not. Just as we arrive on deck to set up our gear, the drizzle returns. It's only light, and there's a tarp above us, holding off most of it, but the occasional wet drift catches us. Harry curses as he pegs a sheet of plastic over his keyboard, then burrows his hands underneath to reach the keys. I'm just glad I thought to bring a jacket to wear over my sundress.

It's freezing, but it seems every passenger has turned up, hopeful in summer clothing, to watch the ship sail out of the harbour. The buzz of anticipation is amazing. It's like a scene from a movie – the vastness of the ship towering over the pier, the deck chairs surrounding the pool, the throbbing of the vessel as it eases out of the port, and of course the promise of sunshine, beaches and happiness. How lucky am I?

As the ship approaches the Sydney Harbour Bridge, the crowd goes eerily quiet. There's an intensity of concentration. Will we fit underneath? It doesn't look like it. We're all holding our breath. And then a humungous cheer erupts as the ship's funnel clears the underside of the structure. Ridiculous, but I'm grinning with the joy of it.

We pass the Sydney Opera House – we're sailing! – and people lined up all around the iconic building's rails wave at us. We wave back madly, cheering. The ship's horn blares, and everyone jumps with fright, then laughter ripples through the crowd. Harry and I start up Dobie Gray's "Drift Away". It seems the perfect song for this moment. I'm trying to absorb the scene as I sing, to store it in my memory as something amazingly special. Something not everybody gets to do. In this moment, I can forget about everything. About

Snap. About home. All the things that have been bringing me down.

Music is literally taking me places.

20

Vexation

Later that night as we're getting ready for our evening gig, the gloss suddenly wears off. Although the cabin's stench has been replaced by sweet-smelling carpet deodoriser, when I step out of the shower, I discover a bigger problem. I search the tiny bathroom with its shallow-mirrored cabinets and non-existent drawers, telling myself I must be going blind. Eventually, I have to accept what I'm looking for is just not here. Wrapped head to toe in towels, I stick my face through the bathroom doorway.

"Are you kidding me?"

Harry looks up from his laptop, mouth open in surprise. "What?"

"There's no hair dryer!" I spot the drawers in the desk that runs along the cabin wall and step out to check them. No luck.

"Really?" asks Harry.

"Really, truly, freakin' dead set. What sort of cruise ship is this? The website said every room has a hairdryer."

"Uh... I don't use one. I didn't notice. Maybe that's just the passenger rooms?"

"Well, can we get one? Can we ask Thomas?"

He grimaces. "I don't actually know how to contact him. He just turns up to clean the room every morning. I can ring the service desk."

He reaches for the phone, and I wait behind him while he talks. I'm suddenly conscious of my nakedness beneath the towels. Harry doesn't seem to notice. He hangs up and pulls a sad face.

"Sorry. Hairdryers are all pre-installed."

"Argh. Not in here they're not. What is this? Peasant division? What about the gift shop?"

"Nope."

"For fuck sake. What—"

"Fruit sake." He flinches at my I'm-going-to-kill-you expression.

I drag the towel off my head and point to my wet tangle. "What am I supposed to do with this?" I no longer care if he sees me in a mess. He should have told me.

He sighs. "Ponytail? Gel?"

"Thanks."

I stomp back to the bathroom, stubbing my toe on the bottom rim of the doorway. It's a few centimetres high, designed to stop water spillage. It's also perfectly designed for busting toes. I curse again and slam the door behind me. Okay, I should have brought my own dryer. I had thought about it, but when Harry said I needed to avoid excess luggage fees, I left it out to make room for the other stuff in my solitary suitcase. Crap. I'm being a princess, I know, but my nerves are getting the better of me.

A ponytail, he says. I don't have enough length to catch it all up, and if I let it dry naturally it'll be Frizz City. I have to try something. Maybe a wet gel look isn't such a bad idea. I set to work rubbing my hair as dry as I can with the towel, then try slicking it back with product. Not too shabby.

"Sleek," Harry says, when I emerge. "Sexy."

His arse is saved.

We have our dinner at what the crew call "The Trough". It's the ship's buffet but not as bad as it sounds. The food is hot and tasty, even if mass-produced.

"We're on in about twenty," Harry says.

I nod, scraping the last bit of chocolate mousse from my little metal cup. "Uh huh. Do you think I could have a shot of brandy?"

He looks surprised. "When did you start drinking that?"

"Paul bought me one at the casino, with honey. Took the edge off."

Harry doesn't look happy. What's it to him? "It's for my throat." Why am I justifying myself? He's not the boss of me.

"Okay. Just one. We're not supposed to drink while we're working. After is fine. Just go easy 'cos everything we buy is tracked on our purchase cards."

The lounge is buzzing with conversation when we arrive. I'm buzzing too: I sculled my brandy — not an easy task in the big balloon glass they served it in. Now I'm tipsy, rather than nervy. We work through our first set, and it's obvious no-one's in a dancing mood; it's been a long day and people want to chill and chat. Fine with me. We stick to laid back material for the next two sets. There'll be plenty of time for partying in the days to come.

Close to 1 am, done and dusted, we carry our equipment back to the room. My throat is burning, my shoulders are aching, and I'm bumping into walls with the swaying of the ship. There's a dull ache in my stomach too. I hope I'm not getting seasick. I should probably dose up again with Travacalm.

"How're you feeling?" asks Harry. "You look a bit pale."

I go to speak, and my voice sticks. He looks at my pained expression and returns it with a sympathetic one.

"Throat?"

I nod, pouting.

"You did really well to get through two gigs in one day with a cold. I can imagine how wrecked you're feeling."

His sympathy helps.

"Shipwrecked," I croak, managing a smile. "Bed."

I hope he doesn't think that's an invitation. Don't be stupid. If I look anything like I feel, he wouldn't touch me with a double pair of roadie gloves. Harry dumps his chart folder on the floor and digs in his pocket for the keys.

"A cup of lemon tea, two Panadol, then straight to sleep for you," he says.

"You've got lemon tea?"

"Yep. Swiped it from The Trough at breakfast this morning. Pinched some honey pots too. Thought you might need them."

I nearly swoon. What an angel. We enter the room and dump our gear in a corner. I collapse onto my bed, fake a snore into my pillow, then sit up coughing. Bad idea, it killed my throat.

Harry laughs. "Wait until you've had a week of late nights and early mornings."

I groan. "We don't have to get up early do we?"

"Not tomorrow. But the day after we'll reach one of the islands, and not even a paralytic drunk can sleep through the anchor dropping."

I push myself upright. "Think I'll have a shower."

Harry nods. "Good idea. I'll make your tea."

The solid water pressure massages my aches. I turn the heat up until my skin tingles. So relieving, except the plastic curtain keeps sticking to my wet butt. A few minutes of bliss, then ... holy shit. My period has come early. Have I upset the gods of the sea or something? That explains why I'm feeling so crap on top of my cold. Definitely not going to be any action the next few days, sick or not.

I hop out of the shower, reach for my tampons in the shallow cabinet. The toilet has a warning sign not to flush disposables. Geez, am I going to have to leave obvious little packets in the bin for Harry to see? This is feeling like a date from hell.

The ship's swaying is getting worse. I hold one hand against the wall to balance myself as I brush my teeth, then sit on the loo while I rub at my mascara. It's a chore, but I don't want Harry to see me panda-eyed in the morning. I change my clothes, whacking my elbow on a ledge. I imagine Harry outside, chuckling at my muffled swearing. I'm going to be covered in bruises before the trip is over. It's a good thing we don't have a swear jar. I'd go broke.

I open the door a fraction to see Harry with his face buried in his laptop. Wishing I'd had time to invest in something classier than a white t-shirt and undies, I quickly pass behind him, clamber into my bed and pull the covers up around my neck.

"Comfy?" he asks.

I nod, then sit up as he points to the tea and Panadol on my bedside table.

"Don't worry about the thin blanket," he says. "The temperature hardly varies down here in the dungeon."

He watches me sip my tea for moment, then stretches and goes to the bathroom. He comes out still fully dressed and sits on the edge of my bed. "I'm just going down to the staff office to check my emails. Connection's usually slow so I might be a little while."

"Mmmm."

He strokes my hair. "Feeling a little better?"

"Mmmm."

He takes my empty teacup and places it on the dresser. I yawn. He waits for me to settle, then leans in and kisses my forehead. "I'll turn the overhead light off," he says pressing the nightlight on the wall next to his own pillow. "Get some sleep. I'll try not to wake you when I come back."

I push in my earplugs, my eyelids already drooping as he pulls the privacy curtain around my bunk. I snuggle down like a pampered but sick child.

Darkness. It takes me a moment to remember where I am. A sudden thump and lurch nearly throws me out of bed. "What the hell?" I reach around and flick the nightlight switch. The curtain is still around my bed. I shove it aside and check the time on my phone. It's just after 4 am. Another thump jolts me. I take my earplugs out.

"Harry?"

He stirs above me, his voice thick with sleep. "Must have hit a squall. You okay?"

"No, I'm scared. What's that thumping?"

"It's just waves."

"Seriously? It feels like we're hitting semi-trailers."

"Mmm."

"Should I be worried?"

Harry laughs and sticks his head over the edge of his bunk. "Do you want me to come down and hold you?"

I look up into his face, considering it. "No, it's okay. I don't want you to catch my cold."

"I'm pretty sure with me being around you all day, that boat's already sailed. Excuse the pun."

I groan. He rolls back on his mattress. The ship continues to sway heavily. I'm waiting for the next thump. When it comes, I have to hold onto the built-in drawers next to my bed to stop being thrown off the mattress. "Far out!"

"Hang on, I'm coming down."

His bunk creaks, and I consider objecting, but I'm really scared. He climbs down and stands next to my bed. "Shove over," he says.

"Um, do you mind climbing in behind?" I ask. "I might... need the loo."

"You feeling sick?"

"Um... no. I might just need it."

It's a good thing there's only the dim glow of the nightlight: my face must be red as hell. I should just tell him. Periods are perfectly natural. Nothing to be ashamed of. But still. What if I have an accident? Would he be grossed-out? Bad luck, he's here now. I hop out so he can get in first, then sidle back in. He pulls the covers over us and wraps an arm around me. The warmth of his body feels good against my back, comforting, until he nuzzles my neck.

"You smell good," he says.

I grimace, trying to fight the quickening of my pulse, the queasiness in my stomach. He kisses my ear.

"Look," I say, flipping the covers back and jumping out again. I stand, arms crossed, but lose my balance and dignity when the ship sways again. "Nothing's happening tonight."

He looks shocked. "I didn't mean..."

"I'm sick."

"I know. It's okay."

"It's not okay."

He stares, puzzled. I owe him an explanation, but it's too embarrassing. I've never talked to a boy about my period. But I don't want him to think I'm rejecting him for no reason. I want to see if this thing can work between us, and I know sex has to be part of it – that's normal, even if I don't know if I'll ever enjoy it or be able to even go through with it – but not now.

"It's not the right time," I mumble.

"It's okay. We don't have to." He pats the bed. "Come back. I won't do anything. I'm sorry if I upset you."

"It's not you. It's…" Oh, stuff it. "I've got my period."

"Ohhh." He points to his bunk. "Do you want me to go back?"

I shrug. "It's up to you."

He shrugs back. "I'm okay, if you are."

Is he just being nice? He's not grossed-out?

"Come back, you goose. You're shivering."

I climb back in, and he covers me up, wrapping his arm around me again but not pressing up so tight. "Sleep," he says. Now I'm so conscious of his closeness, it takes me ages to relax, even though it feels nice to be held. Real nice.

Thump.

I close my eyes and try some deep breathing exercises. I conjure a clear blue sky without a wisp of a cloud. Clarity. Harmony. Tranquillity. It's no use, my mind meanders. I wonder how Snap is doing and how his grandmother is treating him. I hope they've found some peace with each other. I think of Mum. There's no reason I can't visit her now. And I want to. I just don't know if going back to Wineera is a good idea, or how I'll react when I get there. It'd be nice to see Mary though. I owe her a visit. Actually, I owe her a lot more than that; she's had my back all this time. How I can repay her?

Thump.

Stop thinking. I try to imagine warm water lapping at white sand, the distant sound of gulls calling, palm trees. I think through every sailing, water, beach or holiday-themed song I've ever heard: "We Are Sailing", "The Love Boat", "My Heart Will Go On", "Six Months in a Leaky Boat", "Down Among the Dead Men". This is not going well.

Eventually, my mind floats, coursing through the happenings of the past couple of days. The flight from Melbourne, boarding the ship, the crew I've met, the two gigs we've done. What did I do with my passport and boarding pass? Oh, they're in the inside zip pocket of my Hello Kitty bag, along with ... Samuel's letter.

Holy shit. I can't believe it's still there after all this time. Why haven't I thrown it away? Burned it? It's nothing to do with me anymore. That was someone else's life. Damn it. Now I can't stop thinking about it. Maybe I should read it. I've moved on enough, haven't I? I think I'm ready – to get all the bad things out of my life, right now, so I can move forward without the weight of what the note might or might not say. I mean, what if the right moment never comes along, and I'm stuck with it forever? I should destroy it. Rip it into a million little pieces and let it float away in the wind at sea, like some funeral ceremony with ashes. Or a forgiveness ritual. I like that idea. I picture the pieces picked up and carried on the breeze, then being caught in a cross current and slamming back into my face. That'd be right.

Still, then I'd never know, would I? I think I'll bite the bullet tomorrow. Definitely. It's time. Yes, I'll read it tomorrow. Maybe. Hell, I wish I'd never remembered it.

21

Prescience

Day five and still no hairdryer. It's good to finally feel almost human though. No more trying to sing with a blocked nose and raw throat, then falling into bed like a zombie. The crimson tide has finished too. Oh, happy day. Maybe I'll actually enjoy tonight's performance instead of being fuzzy headed on Codral and lemon, honey and brandy hot toddies (purely medicinal of course).

Harry comes out of the bathroom wearing only his jeans while I'm trying to wrangle my hair into tiny pigtails. I pause, distracted by his bare chest in the mirror.

"Cute," he says.

I go back to my fiddling. "Thanks. It's called innovation in times of desperation."

I peek at his reflection again as he passes behind me. There's a shiny, smooth scar, shaped like a wobbly pear, high on his right shoulder. Curious. I haven't actually seen his chest naked before, except in the dark, and our moment of intimacy back home wasn't exactly conducive to exploring skin. Nor have these past few days been, because of my face full of snot and riding the cotton pony. Not appetising – for either of us, I suspect, as he hasn't given me more than a cheek or forehead peck since the night of the squall. Is it time to start sending signals?

"This?" he asks, noticing I'm fixated on his scar.

I'm fearful he's going to tell me a horror childhood story, like Snap's. We can't all have them, surely?

"I was five, running around the backyard with no shirt," he says. "Decided I wanted to help with the BBQ. Dad said no, I said yes, whacked a bratwurst on the hot plate. Bam! Landed right in the fat catcher and sprayed me. I bawled all the way to the hospital."

"Oh, poor pet. You won't do that again." Even as I say it, I'm flinching at how much it must have hurt.

"What? No sympathy? I was just a little kid."

How can I not know this about him? All those years we spent growing up through high school, and there are still mysteries about him. He drags his shirt on with a hint of a smirk. He knows I'm watching. I don't care. I'm enjoying the view.

I point out that his face still has a little boy sweetness about it. "You would have been an adorable kid, all giggles and cheekiness."

"Don't think my parents thought so. The term "terrible twos" was invented for me."

I don't believe him. Look at his messy wet hair and fresh-from-the-shower flushed cheeks. So appealing. So hot.

I pop a sparkly pink cowgirl hat on my head. It's Country and Western night, and we've borrowed some props from the ship's theatre. I'm wearing jeans, high heels and a checked shirt that I've tied and untied in front half a dozen times because I can't decide if I look like a Barbie, or a trashy Kim Kardashian. I stand in front of the mirror, still not sure I'm comfortable with my midriff showing.

"You look great," Harry says.

"Mmm. I dunno. I feel a bit ..."

"Sexy?"

"Not really the word I was looking for."

"Hot?"

I laugh. "Not really. It's not too ... slutty?" I untie the shirt and let it hang. It looks daggy. I tie it up again, trying to show less skin.

"If you got it, flaunt it, I say."

"You're not a girl."

"This is true." He comes up behind me and puts his hands on my hips. "But if I was, and I had this beautiful body. I wouldn't let anyone else tell me otherwise."

Oh, the shivers his touch gives me. I could lean back onto his chest, into his arms and let him prove exactly how beautiful he thinks I am, but I turn and push him away. "Paws off, buddy. We got a show to do."

Harry doesn't say anything, and I can't read his face. Am I blowing this? It's the third time this week I've brushed him off. At first, I wanted to wait until I was feeling healthy and my visitors had passed. But now I've run out of excuses, and I'm still holding off. He knows it, I know it. I think the anticipation might have us both on edge. How do I explain how much I want this, but I'm frightened my body will betray me?

Harry slips on a fringed waistcoat and chucks an old fedora on his head. They don't scream cowboy, but they were all that were left after the rest of the crew got to the costume stash. "Okay, let's go," he says. I gulp down what will probably be my last hot toddy. That worries me too: the brandy has been taking the edge off my performance nerves.

We carry our gear down the corridor, not a lot, just bits and pieces that could be easily stolen or mucked about with: Harry's charts, my cordless microphone, iPad and stuff.

"Why don't you put your sheet music onto an iPad too? There must be an app for it," I ask.

Harry wrinkles his nose. "I like old school."

"Old fart, more like it."

I bump him against the wall. He almost loses his balance with the sway of the ship. "Careful!" he chides.

Geez, what's up with him? "Grumpy much?" I try to bump him again, but he evades me.

"Stop it." He moves ahead of me.

"You stop it." I say, chasing him down the hall.

"Quit it." He's running now.

"Spell cantankerous geriatric."

Finally, I get a laugh out of him. "Okay, barley. We're going to break something."

In the lounge, Harry sits at the piano, warming up his fingers with a few runs. I set up my mic, link up my iPad to the mixing desk, then sound check. All good, we launch into our first bracket.

It's feeling sweet until I notice a dude at the bar full-on staring at me. He's obviously with a girl and another couple, but he keeps eyeing me. I beam a smile, trying to distract his gaze, letting him know I'm aware of him. Does he even know he's being creepy? He doesn't react, just keeps staring. Maybe he's short-sighted, can't really see me at all — that lost-in-thought thing. I ignore him and focus my attention on the other side of the room.

Harry launches into "Thank God I'm a Country Girl". Thank god for Google and looking up lyrics. Never in a million years did I think I'd be singing this, but there you go, you gotta do what you gotta do. Even though the ship's internet is slow as, I managed to get the lyrics for this song and five more. We're going to have to intersperse the country songs between our usual stuff or repeat them as punters come and go.

Creepy dude is still staring as Harry and I reach our first break, so I head to the other end of the bar to get us some water. The stools are a little high for me, so I have to hoist myself up. My legs dangle. The guy next to me is telling his mate, "Gonna get pissed. Can't do it sober." I hate to think what he's planning.

I can't help it, maybe it's an instinctual thing, but I glance back at Creepy Dude. He's moved a few seats closer, and he's doing that slow head to toe thing on my body. I pull my shirt down over my stomach a bit, but it reveals too much of my cleavage. I pull it back up. Why did I wear something so skimpy? What was I thinking? I wish he'd stop staring. How do other girls look so confident when they wear this stuff? Do they like being eye-raped? Because that's what it feels like.

The waiter puts the water on the bar. He's over-filled the glasses, so I have to try and slip off the stool without spilling them. Creepy Dude is suddenly there. He reaches and grabs me by the waist, lifting me off the stool and placing me on the floor. It all happens in a couple of seconds, but with the amount of sensory information my brain processes, it feels much longer: the hotness of his hands on my exposed skin, the meatiness of his fingers digging into my flesh, the strength of his arms controlling my movement.

"Take your hands off me!" I yell.

He lets go, but I'm tingling with revulsion, as if a python had coiled its scaly, muscular body around me.

Everyone turns to look.

He steps back, hands in the air. "I was just trying to help."

"I didn't ask you to," I spit.

His flushed face hardens. "Bloody feminist."

"Well, if being a feminist means I don't put up with creeps like you checking out my body, then deciding they're entitled to grab it without my permission, I'm fine with that."

He flounders. I stand my ground, pulse pounding in fight or flight mode, daring him to deny it. This guy is one second away from wearing two glasses of water.

Harry is suddenly by my side. "What's going on?"

I shove the drinks at Harry. "Nothing. Just some jerk. It's over."

I storm back to the stage to get my purse. When I turn back, Harry is talking to the creep. They're gesticulating, but I can't hear what they're saying. He comes over to me, looking concerned. "Are you okay?"

"No, I'm not. Some people should learn to keep their hands to themselves."

"I don't think he meant any harm."

I blink at him, not believing what he's said. "You're taking his side?"

"I'm not taking sides, I'm just trying—"

"He manhandled me."

"He said he was just trying to help ... Hey! Where are you going?"

I'm out of there. So furious I can hardly speak. I grind my words out over my shoulder. "Start without me."

Every person I pass in the hallway is like a barrier. I grit my teeth so I don't yell at them to get out of my way. The lift is busy, so I pound down the stairs instead. Once I reach level four, I pause. There's another lounge here. No, I can't get drunk; the alcohol will show on my purchase card. There's nowhere else to go but our room, or overboard, and the latter doesn't appeal.

I sit on the edge of my bunk hugging myself. Furious. Vice-like pain in my shoulders. How could Harry not defend me? Couldn't he see the guy was a jerk? And even if he couldn't see, my word should have been enough. The guy handled me, put his filthy, hot hands on my skin. I bet it was caught on camera. Maybe the powers that be will investigate. What happens if I don't go back out there? I'll be the second girl Harry has had to let go. That won't look good. Have I ruined things for him? Still, I shouldn't have to put up with jerks.

I wish I'd snuck a bottle of vodka into my suitcase. I've heard other crew mention they've filled water bottles with alcohol. I sigh. How do I deal with this? When Harry touched my waist earlier, his hands stirred something sensual, warm, but another guy touches me and whammo, I'm freaked out. I should have brushed it off, politely told him to fuck the hell off, then got on with my job. Then I think back, yet again, to that night in Harry's bed when my body betrayed me. What the hell is going on inside me? Why can't I be normal? Other girls my age are having fabulous sex lives. Aren't they?

What to do? I glance around the room — at my backpack, the drawers, Harry's clothing hanging on a hook, my purse beside me on the bed ... Wait! And the answer appears. Just like that.

I pull open my purse, dig down to the bottom, and there it is. The plastic baggy. I pull it out, hold it up to the light. The tablet is still in one piece. Still pink. I pick out the tablet and place it in my palm. What if it's not an E? It might make me sick. But Paul took one. He was fine.

Should I?

No. I'm being stupid. I poke it back inside my purse and go to the toilet. Anything for a distraction. I can't help but stare at myself in the mirror while I sit. I'm haggard. Not what a healthy eighteen-year-old girl should look like. When did this happen? I wipe, flush, wash my hands, then rub at my smudged eyeliner. I didn't even realise I'd been crying. Freakin, crying, crying, crying. I thought I was past that. Life was supposed to be getting better now. I'm sick of it.

Screw it. I'm taking the E.

Here I go, sitting on the bed, tablet in hand. There's a noise outside the door. Harry? I snatch my hand closed, ready to shove the tablet back in my purse. I wait. Whoever it is keeps on moving past.

I open my palm again. The tablet's surface looks like cracked earth, worn from where it's been in my mouth before. Does E have a use-by date? What's it going to feel like? I wonder if Harry will be able to tell I took something. My hand shakes as I pick up the tablet with my thumb and forefinger. It's smaller than I remember. I take a breath. Am I doing this? Yes. I place it on my tongue, grab the water bottle from my bedside drawer. Sip. It's gone. Too late for regrets.

I wait for some sort of buzz. Nothing. I lie back, breathe deep, let my mind skim over the last few nights. They've been great: a few nerves but nothing major. I'd say I've actually been enjoying myself. Coming into my own at last. Then tonight. Did I overreact? I don't think so. I mean, what made that guy think it was okay to grab me like that? But ... maybe I shouldn't have yelled.

Maybe I shouldn't have smiled at him.

I get up and examine my image in the mirror. Okay, let's be honest — the clothes are showing too much for my liking. I knew that before I went out there. But the internet is full of women telling me to be proud of my body, my sexuality, to be comfortable with myself, to be myself, that dressing like this is not slutty, not asking for it. It's owning it. How do I come to terms with that? What's wrong with being attractive? Is that why this keeps happening to me? Is being attractive asking for it? Sigh. Look at me. I'm doing the very thing I said I wasn't going to do: selling my body as part of the package.

It hits me then, the truth: my lack of confidence isn't about my voice, my performance. I'm past that now. It's about being looked at. The way Samuel looked at me that night.

He's still alive in every man out there.

I glance at my backpack. Visualise his unopened letter, the words ... reminding me. Am I ready for that? No. But it could be the answer to this paranoid nightmare in my head.

Harry is halfway through a song and looking unhappy when I get back, but I'm finding it hard to care; my body is buzzing nicely, my head in a cloudy place. I squeeze onto the piano stool next to him, try to look contrite. "Sorry."

"You okay?"

I nod, smile, watch his hands on the keys, the way they drift effortlessly from note to note, like they're independent beings, separate to him. He winds up his song, and I grab my mic. "Let's do this."

Four songs in, it really hits me: a wall of adoration rolling in from the audience and whooshing through every atom in my body. Every song is a symphony. Every lyric an opera. And I'm the coolest, hippest, hottest chick that ever strutted a stage. Look at me sing! Look at me dance! I'm all curves and sass. Shaking that thing.

The room is filling up with post-dinner passengers. I'm pumped because this lot is animated, up for a dance. Great.

So am I. I wander about the dance floor as I sing, down through the lounges, getting up close and personal. One guy offers me a shot of something clear. Vodka? Sambuca? How can I refuse? It's a party. Somewhere inside, I might be vaguely aware that this confident, sassy chick isn't me, but I don't care. I'm along for the ride for as long as it lasts.

During our next break a crew member calls a bingo game. I want to participate, keep the fun going, but Harry drags me away. He's still not looking happy. Glowering even. I grab him in a big hug and tell him how grateful I am to be working with him. How much I love performing with him. I add a sneaky, "Do you want to go back to our room?"

His response isn't what I expect. "Stop it. What are you doing?"

"What do you mean?"

"You're acting crazy. Are you on something? Coke?"

I give him a wide-eyed look. "What? I'm just having fun, doing what I love. This is my drug." I wave my arms to encompass the room. Then I whisper, all conspiratorial, "Some guy just gave me a couple of shots of tequila. I figured why not. I deserve it after that jerk. Sue me."

He shakes his head. "Settle. You don't want us kicked off in your first week, do you? Whatever you do reflects on both of us."

I attempt a solemn look. "No, sir."

"I'm not kidding. Every room is monitored. You can't get away with anything here."

"Well, that's fine by me. They'll be able to see what happened wasn't my fault."

I grin, but I'm losing the battle. Harry takes my hand. "Come on, let's go for a walk. Get some air. We've got some time to kill before the next bracket."

"Whatevs."

We head to one of the outside decks and stroll towards the bow. I feel like skipping, but I control myself. We watch the ocean, lit up by the ship's lights, the waves breaking into sparkly, foamy showers. A few metres out, the world is a black undulating blanket, except for where the moon is casting a shivering trail. It's the stuff of fairy tales. The air's humid, and I close my eyes, throw my head back and let the ever-present breeze blow over my body. It's like being wrapped in warm fairy floss.

Sighing, I lift Harry's arm and snuggle under like a duckling. "Life is good."

"It's not fame and fortune, but it's okay, hey?" he says.

I nod, fuzzy with affection. "The best." I lift my face, hoping for a kiss. It doesn't arrive.

"Don't blow it," he says, his eyes out to sea instead of on me.

I pout. Big deal. My body is happiness itself and nothing and no-one can disappoint me right now.

We head back in. The bingo is still being called, albeit constantly interrupted by a raucous American couple who have been here since the start of the night. Now they're jolly with alcohol, laughing and yelling out numbers to confuse people. It's all being taken in good spirit.

Towards midnight, there's still about forty people hanging around, but the dance floor is empty except for the Americans who are doing some amazeball moves to our pop music. We finish our final song and begin saying goodnight when, on cue, up comes the predictable drunken dude wanting "one more song". He stumbles as he approaches and steadies himself by grabbing my mic stand. I step back, not wanting a microphone-shaped hole in my teeth. "Do-ya play that Joe Cocker thing? You know the "hat" song?"

I look at Harry, who's unplugging his keyboard. He shakes his head. "Sorry. It's pack-up time."

"Ahhh, go on mate, it's for my spessshal lady." He leans in close, and I reel back from the intensity of his breathy fumes. "Gonna propose, mate. You gotta help me out."

My loving heart can't help itself. "Ohhh." I raise my eyebrows at Harry. "Come on, we can't let him down."

Harry slumps his shoulders. "At least it's not Nine Inch Nails or Chisel," he says under his breath.

"Sure, we can do that," I tell the dude.

He immediately turns and yells. "Mish! Mishy!"

Mishy is sitting with another couple. She has pale pink lipstick and red shoulders with white strap marks. She's done a good job getting burned even though it's been overcast every day since we left. Dedication, I expect. She looks tired, sucking on her Margarita. She doesn't want to get up.

"What?" she yells back.

"Com'ere," he says, beckoning to her.

He gets down on one knee and nods to us. We start the song, and he begins to unbutton his shirt. Oh god, what did we get ourselves into? Mishy comes forward, all giggly in her bright pink sarong and braided hair.

"Oh my god!" she squeals.

They have the room's attention. Drunk dude has his shirt off, and he's swinging it above his head. One minute he's gyrating his hips, getting into it, the next a security bouncer the size of a truck is standing beside him, arms crossed, feet squared. "Put it back on," he says. The bouncer glares at us, and we don't have to be told twice. Music off.

The drunk grins. "Just a bit of fun, mate."

The bouncer doesn't budge. The drunk dresses himself, gives the bouncer a good-natured salute and returns to his friends and beer. He seems to have forgotten what he came to do. Game over. Poor Mishy will have to wait.

It's bedtime. But the happiness fairy has stolen all my sleepiness. I like being this open, this free, this not giving a care about being in my t-shirt and undies. Harry's at his computer with his headphones on. And there's his beautiful, wide shoulders begging for my hands to massage them.

"Feel good?" I ask, attempting a husky voice.

"Mmmm?" He can't hear.

I lift one side of his headphones and whisper into his ear. "What are you doing?"

He takes off his headphones, snaps his computer closed and stands. "Working on a new song."

"For moi?" I ask, all cutesy.

"We'll see."

I glance at my bunk. It's got stuff all over it: clothes, make-up, brochures, papers. Crap. I don't remember doing that. I gather everything in my arms. Some of it lands on the floor, the rest in a heap on a chair. I throw back the bedcovers, hop in and pat the mattress.

Harry's watching. He shoves his hands in his pockets. "I gotta check my emails while it's quiet down there. Might be a while. Don't wait up for me." He grabs the room key and heads out. Not even a goodnight kiss.

What the hell? Was that the world's most devastating brush-off or what? I grab a book, punch my pillows into comfort and slump back. I read the same paragraph four times, then slap the book down and put my earbuds in, listen to music – loud, crashy stuff. It's not the same. The happiness fairy has done a runner. Magic carpet ride over. Joy no longer courses through my veins and muscles, speaking to me in a language I can only feel, not comprehend. I turn the music off, lie still, just breathing, the grumble of the ship's engine far below in the belly of the vessel.

I wake up in the dark. It's around 5.30 am. Harry's bunk is empty, so I snap the main light on. The room is clean, my clothes are folded on a chair, and my make-up is tucked away in the bathroom. What a dork. A sweet, sweet dork.

22

Latency

I dress in shorts and a t-shirt, wash my face, dampen and scrape my hair back, then wander up to the top deck. It's a hazy dawn, but the clouds have relented, and we're going to have a clear day. In between gusts of wind, the air is warm and sticky with salt. Only a couple of other early birds are up: an older couple in tracksuits, jogging laps of the walking track.

In the distance is the voluptuous silhouette of a large island. Port Vila. It's the first stop on this trip where the ship can actually dock. That means we'll get a whole day off the ship. Until now, at the smaller islands, we've had to wait for all the other passengers to board tenders before we could get off – the non-perks of being entertainers. Still, chilling, swimming and flaking on an island beach for half a day each stop has been such a hard life. It's just a shame that today I feel as if I'm dragging around the ship's anchor instead of my body.

I find Harry sitting alone in the main eatery. His hands are wrapped around a coffee mug. He doesn't see me approaching – he's looking out the window at the endless green swells. There's a seagull clinging to the railing outside, its feathers ruffled in the wind. That's something that surprises me about the ship – it's so windy, all the time. Makes sense I guess, with the ship constantly in motion. I had expected day after day of sun, blue skies and gentle breezes. But you have to find yourself a sheltered sun lounge if you don't want a bad hair day, every day.

The hot breakfast buffet isn't ready yet, so I grab a muffin and a juice. Thank god for food 24-7. Harry eyes me as I sit, then returns his gaze to the window.

"We'll be hitting Port Vila pretty soon," he says. "We should do some sightseeing. There's a waterfall worth visiting. The stream is this pale-green milky colour that collects in pools. We can swim."

"Don't go chasing waterfalls..."

"What?"

"Nothing."

I break my muffin apart and offer him a piece. He refuses. "Have you been to bed at all?" I ask through my mouthful.

He shrugs. "A bit."

The muffin sticks in my throat as I swallow. I take a gulp of juice. Harry is now fixated on his coffee. His eyes are puffy and red-rimmed. One of them twitches when he blinks.

"Is it something I've done?" I ask.

"I don't know. You tell me." He holds my gaze.

Oh shit. I'm in trouble. "What?"

"Really?"

"Really. What?"

He sighs and picks up his cup. It's empty. He puts it back down. "Forget it."

I scrape at the crust of muffin stuck to the wrapper, it gathers under my nail, and I have to suck it off. Did I do something stupid last night?

"I don't understand you," he says.

"What's to understand?"

"First you crack it because some guy tries to help you off a stool—"

"That guy was a dick." Well, I remember that.

"Then you come back all wired and flirty, sitting on guys' knees and pinching drinks like you're some crazy cabaret show. I don't get it. What's going on with you?"

"I what?"

He stares at me. Hard. He's serious.

"I don't remember that. I mean, I remember having a great time but ..."

"Did you take something?" he asks. "Tell me the truth."

I can't look at him. "I might have drunk a bit too much, but—"

"You know what? Maybe this is a mistake."

My skin tingles with dread.

He clears his throat. "Maybe we shouldn't—"

"Morning." It's more of a bellow than a greeting. We both turn towards the sliding glass doors leading to the outer deck. It's the couple who were jogging. Now I recognise them as the Americans from last night. "Well, would you look who it is," the guy says. He's bear-like, tall and broad, with curly grey chest hairs escaping over the top of his tracksuit zip.

"Mikey," Harry says.

Mikey heads straight for us and holds out his giant mitt, all pudgy and thick, as if it's made of donuts. Harry's delicate musician's hand disappears inside it. "Didn't think musos got out of bed before midday," he says.

Harry turns on the charm, chuckling. "It's a myth. Don't you believe it."

"Not in my day." Mikey winks at me. "Booze, sex and rock 'n' roll, hey?"

I manage a tense smile.

"Mind if we join you?" he asks.

God, please no. I flash a look at Harry, but Mikey is already pulling out a chair for his wife.

Harry shrugs. "Lauren, you remember Mikey and Marcy, don't you? From last night?"

Is he testing me? I return his glare. "Sure."

Their hair looks as though they've both just rolled out of bed. Marcy runs a hand through hers to flatten it. "Phew, bit blowy out there. But gotta get our jog in, hail or shine..."

She prattles on, but I'm not listening. I'm still smarting from Harry's words, and I need to escape so I can do some thinking. "Excuse me. There's a muffin over there with my name on it."

"I'll join you, honey," Marcy says. "Gotta get some eggs into us. And bacon. You Aussies know how to do a good breakfast. But maple syrup, that's what I'm missing – the real stuff, not that flavoured gunk."

Damn. I was hoping to take my muffin back to the cabin. She links her arm through mine and pulls me along. Where does she get off being so confident? Haven't people on this ship heard of personal space?

At the buffet counter, a chef is adding a giant bowl of Bircher muesli to the rows of packet cereals and plates of cold meats and cheeses. There's a hiss of frying coming from the galley. "Eggs on yet?" she asks.

"I can prepare some for you, madam. What would you like?" His white uniform is crisp, not a speck on it.

Marcy orders two serves of fried eggs, sunny-side up, sausages, bacon and pancakes. Geez, does she eat like this every day? Why isn't she the size of a barn? She elbows me. "Madam? Did you hear that? Haven't been called that since my brothel days." She unzips her tracksuit a little and uses the sides of her arms to squeeze her boobs together. They make a weathered and wrinkly cleavage. "Whaddya reckon? Think I'd still pass?" She cackles. "Oh, look at your face," she says. "I'm joking, honey."

The chef acts as if he hasn't witnessed Marcy's boob action. "I'll bring it to your table will I, madam?"

She winks at him. "Honey, you can bring it to me, anytime, anywhere."

The poor guy nods politely and nobly heads to the kitchen.

Marcy squeezes my shoulder and leans in close. "Okay, I wasn't a hooker, but I was an exotic dancer. Wouldn't believe it, would you?"

My smile is genuine this time. There's something down to earth about her. Something honest. I lean and grab a muffin. It's sitting in my hand. I could just walk away, back to the solitude of the cabin, but I feel strangely obliged to wait with her.

Maybe it's the thought of what she'd write on her passenger feedback form: "Entertainer was a rude bitch". I don't think that's it though. I think I actually like her. She's intriguing. Especially the bit about being a dancer. A mostly naked dancer. I want to pick her brain about that part.

She heads towards the coffee pots, and I follow her like a chick to a mother hen. "Want one? Nothing like the first pot of the day. You know sometimes they don't even empty them as they go along? They just keep topping up the stewed leftovers. True, on my mother's grave." She crosses herself with her hot pink fingernails.

"No. Thanks. I'm okay."

"You know, honey. I saw what happened last night."

Oh shit. Am I in trouble?

"You should have smacked that creep one. Back in my day, we had minders for low-lifes like that. Men weren't allowed to lay a hand on us. If they did, they were out on their butts, probably with a black eye and broken nose."

I smile gratefully. I do like this woman.

"Honey?" She takes my chin and makes me look her in the eye. "Don't you let creeps like that ruin your night. You tell them what's what. And if management gives you any grief you tell them to speak to Marcy. Mikey and I are regulars on this ship. We'll set them straight."

Ironically, it occurs to me that she's touching me without my permission right now. And I question the way she harassed that chef. But her words fill me with grit.

I grin. "Thanks, Mum."

"Cheeky."

She pours her coffee and holds up the pot to check if I've changed my mind. I haven't.

"Marcy? Can I ask you something?"

She returns the coffee pot, then focuses her full attention on me. She has the most beautiful green eyes. They see right through me. Just like a real mum.

"Honey? Why so sad?"

"It's nothing." I swallow. "What I want to know is ... how did you cope with all those men looking at you? I mean, perving at your body? When I'm up there I just want to hide. Because I know what they might be thinking."

Marcy sighs, moves over to a booth and sits. "Come here, honey." She pats the seat next to her. I glance over at Harry. He looks deep in conversation with Mikey. I sit next to Marcy, and she turns to face me. She lifts my hand, and I'm surprised when she places it on my own breast. "Who does this belong to?" she asks.

I frown. Is this a game? "Me."

"Correct."

She moves my hand to my stomach. "Who does this belong to?"

"Me."

My leg. "Me."

My hair. "Me."

When she moves it to rest on my crotch, I blush.

"They're just body parts, right? Your body parts. You were born with them. You own them. They're beautiful. You should be proud of them. Love them."

I nod. Easier said than done.

She continues. "You own the stage when you get up there, too. You have a right to be there. Yes?"

I nod again. But ... Do I?

"Well, if you own the stage and you own your body parts, you're the one in control and no matter what—"

"But they're looking at me that way."

"Lauren, what goes on inside other people's heads is none of your business. You can't control what people think. You can only control how they interact with you. Set boundaries."

"But that guy touched me."

"Yes, I know. He was a creep."

I wait for her to continue but she's just looking at me. That's it? Seriously? "So ... what? I should just get over it?

"This isn't about last night. Am I right?"

Her smile is sad. For me. I can't stand it. This giant lump suddenly fills my throat. I glance back at the coffee machine. Maybe I want some after all.

"Lauren?"

I turn back.

"How long are you going to play victim?"

"What?"

She looks at me hard, and I so much want to look away, but I can't. "Whatever he did to you, whoever "he" is, it shouldn't have happened. Who was he, Lauren? Someone older? Someone you trusted?"

I nod. Blink. Tears are a nanosecond away.

"Breathe," she says.

And I do, I suck in air as if it's the last I'll ever have, hold it deep in my chest.

"That's it. Let it go now, slowly."

She waits for me to exhale. It takes me a while. My throat is so constricted.

"You resent him."

I nod again. There's no chance of speaking right now.

"Maybe even loved him?"

Did I?

"What he did was terrible?"

I purse my lips. Tight. Biting down the terror in my chest.

"But honey, you can't change that. Nothing you do can change it. It was awful and it happened. What you can change is riding that victim train and getting people on board with you. The longer you ride it, the longer you keep giving him your power."

Now I speak 'cos I'm so freaking angry. "I never—"

"I know, I know," she says. "You think I'm blaming you now."

Isn't she?

"But you know in your heart, you're the only one who can change now. Because holding hurt in makes it worse, makes it fester. And if you don't let it go, you'll never be the wonderful, courageous, beautiful person you were meant to be."

Oh god, don't.

"You gotta focus on the people that matter now. Okay? I want you to do two things – for yourself, not for me. I want you to find someone you can open up to." She glances over to Harry. "Whoever they are, you need to be a brave girl and take a leap of faith. Because if you don't ... well, you're always going to feel ashamed, or angry, or scared. And you and I both know ..." she pauses to stroke my cheek, "self-medicating doesn't work."

Blush. Blush. Blush.

"One day at a time. Okay? The other thing I want you to do is look up a self-defence class."

Finally. Something I can do.

"Not just because every girl needs to be able to protect herself, but, honey, it'll give you your power back. Trust me. Okay? You promise?"

I nod, suddenly weighted by my lack of sleep. I'd kill to be hiding under my blankets. In the dark. Where I can process this. Where I can cry it out in private. "Okay," I croak.

Marcy squeezes my hand. We head back to the table, and I find I can't even bite my muffin. The café is filling up, and my head is feeling more sorry for itself by the moment. "I need to crash for a while," I mumble.

"Ah, I told you," Mikey says. "You young folk have no stamina." He smiles at me. "You should eat more. You look like a sparrow," he says. "Piaf, we'll call you."

I have a flash back to that film – the one with that French Marion something-or-other actress – where Piaf is small and crumpled, towards the end of the film. I think I have an inkling of how she felt.

"We'll see you in the lounge tonight, hun," Marcy says, getting up and pressing me to her cleavage, which she's forgotten to zip up. Her perfume smells like the sugared icing on a Boston bun. "Love your work, honey. Wish I could sing like that." Then she whispers, "I'm here if you wanna talk."

Her tenderness makes me want to stay crushed to her. "Thanks," I murmur.

Mikey stands, but Harry is in his way, so I'm spared a bear hug. The big guy waves. "Will you sing some Patsy Cline for us tonight? "Crazy" is our favourite."

For once, I manage to subdue my cynicism and smile. "Sure."

Harry stands too. "I might get going too. I could do with a bit more sleep."

"I knew it," Mikey says. "Up before midday. Bound to happen."

"You got me," Harry says, cocking his finger like a pistol.

We leave them as their fry-ups arrive. In the corridor, I lose my balance, bumping into the wall as the ship sways. Harry tries to put an arm around my shoulder, but I shrug him off. I'm confused. He can't tell me it's over, then touch me like that.

Back in the cabin, I don't bother changing out of my clothes; I just slip my shoes off and get straight into bed. Under the covers, I press my earplugs in and, like a pissed-off Mr Pink, turn my back on Harry.

My eyes are gritty, and I don't think I'm going to sleep with my brain working overtime, but suddenly Harry is patting my arm.

"It's nearly eleven," Harry says. "We should probably get going if you want to see the waterfall."

I scrunch my eyes against the fluoro light. "Urgh. Do we have to?"

"No. Not if you don't want to, but it's your only chance to see it. We'll be moving on tonight."

I consider the option. We still need to sort stuff out between us. I should go. A change of scenery might make things easier. I push my legs out of bed and sit hunched, crusty. He's already showered and dressed. I yawn, tempted to fall back into the covers.

"Have you booked a tour?" I ask. Maybe if he hasn't, I can go back to sleep.

"Don't need to. We just bargain with a taxi driver at the port."

I yawn again, not moving. "Okay, but I'm not swimming. I can't be bothered getting into bathers."

"Come on, snooze-a-lot." He tousles my hair. "I've got us a picnic lunch. Can we use your backpack? Mine's got the towels and stuff in it."

Talk about a mood swing. Last I remember, he was cranky and breaking up with me, even though we're not actually together. Or is that something else I don't remember? I head for the bathroom. Okay, we're going.

Grumpy man is at the security checkpoint again. It makes me wonder if he's a permanent fixture, like a masthead on a ship. Only he's more of a gargoyle. We walk off the gangway right into a local market with every kind of tropical, touristy souvenir known to mankind. I grab a couple of red and yellow hibiscus leis. The synthetic blooms are fraying at the edges. I try to throw one over Harry's head, but he ducks.

"No way."

"Awww, come on, just a bit of fun, maaate," I slur, imitating the drunk dude from last night. Weird. How come I remember him but not what Harry says I was doing?

"The drivers will see us coming. They'll take us for tourists and charge us double."

"We are tourists."

"No, we're not."

I pout. I'm trying to make the most of this. Why can't he? "Come on, let's just have some fun?"

I watch his face. He's scowling as if the decision holds the gravity of taking out a mortgage. He gives in, lets me put the lei on him. "Happy now?" he asks.

I grin. "It suits you."

"I'm sure."

We negotiate a price with a driver and set off through the township with its weathered, white-painted buildings, concrete roads and cracked footpaths. Outside an ice cream shop, a local mother is passing a giant cone to her tiny, fuzzy-haired child. His big eyes and open mouth show joy at the prospect of eating an ice cream almost as big as his head. I make a mental note to stop there on our way back.

As I'm looking out the window, Harry takes my hand. I don't move, just breathe deep, my heart skipping a little. The skin on skin feels good. Warm. Right. Why can't we just be? Why does it have to be so complicated? This on–off, up–down, angry–happy stuff is driving me crazy. It must be driving him crazy too. I grip his hand firmer, letting him know it's okay. Hold on. Surely, we can work it out?

Ten minutes more, and we're out of the central township, heading past shanty houses shrouded in creeping greenery. Further into the countryside, the road is dotted with aged wooden benches next to rotted wooden poles that serve as bus stops.

Our taxi driver, Luke, turns into a gravel parking lot, the handbrake ratcheting as he comes to a halt. We step out into a rainforest, its tall canopy blocking the sun. I sniff the cool air with its mustiness of rotting undergrowth. Apparently, we've arrived at a national park, and there's an entry fee. Australian dollars are fine.

We follow Luke through the jungle, sticking to packed-dirt paths, but stop when a sudden downpour hits. Luke strolls off the path into the jungle and comes back with two giant green leaves. He bends the stem of one and threads it through the leaf, then pops it on my head.

"Nature's umbrella," he says.

Harry shakes his head. "I'm fine."

What a killjoy.

Further along the path, Luke stops and picks up a fallen coconut.

"You know how local people open this?"

I shake my head, expecting him to magically produce a machete and hack off the green husk, but he sets to work with his magnificently perfect white teeth, ripping off sections until he reaches the inner shell. He whacks the nut on a rock, breaking it into pieces and releasing the water. We each suck and chew on a piece as we continue up the hill.

"You know, the water of the coconut can be used for blood transfusions?" he says.

Harry and I look at each other. Really?

"The chemical make-up is similar to blood plasma," Luke adds.

I'm secretly embarrassed. For some reason I expected Luke to be uneducated. Why else would a forty-odd year old man be making a living by scavenging tourist dollars?

"The women, when they cannot breast feed, give the coconut milk to their babies. Lifeblood, we call it. Very nutritious."

I nod, keen to learn more. Luke has probably told these stories a thousand times, but whether they're true or not, and I have no reason not to believe him, they're fresh to my ears. A while later we reach the waterfall. There's another couple standing waist deep in the pool beneath it. They yell and hoot as they dive into the foamy water cascading over their heads. The water in the pool is an incredible milky aquamarine.

"I've never seen anything like it," I say.

Harry smiles. "Told you."

Luke clears his throat. "Okay. You can swim. I will leave you here for two hours? Happy, yes?"

We ask him to have some lunch with us, but he refuses, disappearing back down the track. Harry pulls out a couple of towels from his backpack, and we settle on a mossy patch beside the pool. He points to my Hello Kitty backpack. Inside is crusty ham and cheese sandwiches, water bottles and a couple of pear ciders. I screw up my nose.

"Try it, I think you'll like it," Harry says. "Hair of the dog might help."

I twist off the lid and gulp a couple of mouthfuls. Not too sweet. It's good. A burp escapes me before I think to cover my mouth. We both laugh. I lie on my stomach, enjoying the spray mist from the waterfall drifting onto my hair and shoulders. The other couple pick their way among the underwater rocks and climb up the embankment to dry their feet and get dressed. Pretty soon we're alone with birdsong, the waterfall, rivulets trickling over rocks. I notice more sounds: the rustling of the rainforest canopy, a frog's chirp – or is that a cricket? Do they have crickets in Vanuatu? Or some other strange variation of insect?

I'm still chewing on a big mouthful of sandwich when Harry decides he's ready to swim. He strips off his shirt and flips off his thongs. When he unzips his shorts, I stop chewing. Is he going in naked? No, he's got boardshorts on underneath. He wades out.

"It's perfect," he calls. "You coming in?"

I shake my head. "Later." I point to my tummy. "Might get a cramp."

"Wuss," he yells.

"Whatever."

Harry floats on his back and swishes his arms like one of those two-armed insects – water boatmen – and heads towards the waterfall. I compromise by sitting on a flat rock and dangling my feet in the water. It's perfectly cool, not cold. I close my eyes and let my head drop back. The sun makes bright red patterns behinds my eyelids. I breathe. It might be psychological, but the air seems cleaner, as if it's been filtered by the water and rocks and greenery. My ordinary life seems so far away. I could stay here forever. And ever.

Something touches my foot, and I wrench my legs out of the water, shrieking. It's Harry. He grabs my arm and pulls me into the water. I flounder until I find my footing. The water only comes up to my hips, but I'm soaked.

"You arsehole." I splash him.

"Steady." He laughs.

"My clothes. I've got nothing to change into."

I look down. My nipples erect against my white t-shirt. I cross my arms, and spin away, heading towards the embankment.

"Stay," he says.

I turn back and glare at him. If looks could kill, he'd be floating face down like a... a... I don't know what. A dead floaty thing. I hoist myself onto a rock and pull my t-shirt away from my body, twisting and squeezing the material until water runs out of it.

He floats off on his back again.

"Arsehole," I repeat under my breath.

At least the sun is my friend. I stay on my rock, feet dangling in the water. The murkiness my thrashing stirred up has settled, and tiny fish nibble at invisible morsels in the gravel. The water is soothing. I could get back in, I suppose, since I'm already wet. Harry looks like he's really enjoying himself ...

No. I get up and head over to our towels, lie on my back, my arm across my face. I bat at a pesky fly that keeps landing on my arm until I realise it's not a fly – it's the little hairs on my arms prickling as they release moisture to the sun. I'm almost asleep when Harry grunts as he climbs out of the water. He drops soggily onto his towel.

"You okay?" he asks.

I squint at him. "Mmmm."

"You pissed at me?"

"Maybe." I close my eyes. The sun makes patterns behind my lids.

"We're even then."

I ignore him, but secretly I'm a bit relieved.

"Hungry?" he asks.

"Hmmm. Not really."

"Not even for chocolate-coated raspberries?"

I open an eye. "Really?"

"They might be a bit melted. Still taste good though."

He breaks open the packet and holds it out to me. I pick one out. He's right, the coating is soft and squishy in my fingers. I pop it into my mouth. It's good. Really good. The raspberry centre is tart and unexpectedly crispy.

"Freeze-died," he says. "Yum, hey?"

I nod, sucking chocolate off my fingers.

He leans back on his elbows, clears his throat, and I just know he wants to talk about last night again.

"I wonder how Snap's doing," I slip in.

"Did you email him?"

"Yeah. He hasn't said much though. I suspect he's grudgingly accepting his granny. He's too big-hearted to turn anyone away. It must be confusing though, being told rubbish about her by his dad all these years."

"He's not the only one who's confused."

"Huh?"

"Last night."

"Ugh." I turn over, bury my face in my towel, muffling my whinge. "Now?"

He doesn't answer.

I huff, sit up and cross my legs, ready to get this elephant out of the way. "Look, I had a bad experience when I was young. And it ... kind of screwed me up. So, when that guy grabbed me, I freaked out." I watch his expression for any sign of judgement. There's none. He nods, keeps looking at me, waiting.

"What? What else do you want? An apology?"

"No. I want to know what happened afterwards."

"I told you, I freaked out. That's it."

His face hardens. He knows. There's no point lying. I should just rip the bandaid off.

"I took an E."

He doesn't react, just sits back and looks out at the water.

"So?" I prompt. Why doesn't he say something?

"Why?"

I throw my hands up. "I don't understand half of what I do myself. I think I'm okay and this ... this huge fear grips me. And I hate myself for it, because ... I wish I could be calm and normal like other people and not fly off the handle. But dudes ... they all think the same, don't they?"

He turns to me. "That's unfair."

"Is it? Tell me. A lone woman walking on Chapel Street at two-thirty in the morning. She's gang raped and left in an alley. What's your first thought?"

"I don't know ..."

"Yes, you do. Just tell me the what pops into your head."

He winces. "It's terrible. It shouldn't happen to anyone. But ... I guess I'd wonder what she was doing there at that time, alone?"

"See? You just proved my point. Why not ask what the men were doing there? And why they felt they had the right to attack the woman? If you read that newspaper report it'll tell you what she was wearing, if she'd been drinking, insinuate she might have been a prostitute. And that negates what happened to her? Does it? Look at Jill Meagher. Look at Eurydice Dixon. They were just trying to get home after a night out, and some creep on the street rapes and murders them. Girls are judged all the time by how they look, what they wear, where they are, how they act."

"Whoa. Where is all this coming from?"

"That guy last night. He had no right to touch me."

"You think he grabbed you because ... what? Because of what you were wearing? He said he was just trying to help you off your chair."

"I didn't need his help. And if he really wanted to help, he should have offered to hold my drinks, not manhandled me."

"Uh huh."

Harry doesn't look convinced. I grind my teeth, breathe, try to speak calmly, but it's hard. This shit makes me furious, probably because I don't have all the answers myself.

"Didn't you see the way he was staring at me during our first bracket? I didn't know which way to look."

"No. You should have told me."

"And you would have done what?"

"Spoken to him at least."

"Seriously? You couldn't even call him out when I told you he grabbed me."

He rubs his hand through his hair. At least I've got him thinking.

"And what if I were to go for a walk on the top deck at midnight? Get some fresh sea air after our gig, and he turns up? How are you gonna save me then? Would you tell me I should have stayed in our cabin, like a good little girl, and have never ventured out? And why should you have to fight my battles, anyway? My word should be enough."

"Because you're not ready to fight your own yet?"

Ooh, I want to smash him.

He holds up his hands. "Hear me out."

This should be good.

"It's obvious there's something upsetting you—"

"No shit, Sherlock."

"Can I speak?"

I purse my lips, dig my nails into my palms. I should shut up.

"Thank you." He clears his throat, looks away, collecting his thoughts or calming himself. "The way you want to be close with me, then don't; your lack of confidence on stage – even though you're brilliantly talented; how easily you want to escape with alcohol; and drugs now. You gotta talk to me about it. Or talk to someone. Or this, we, are going to fall apart."

Oh, that's not fair turning it back on me. My throat thickens so much it's painful, and suddenly I'm spent. "I can't. I just can't," I whisper. There's no fixing this. I am who I am.

"Lauren, look at me."

I shake my head, play with the corner of my towel. Breathe.

"Please? I want to talk to you. Face to face."

I shake my head. I'm not ready.

He taps my knee. "Come on." He takes both my hands. "I think it's time to talk about Samuel."

I think I've heard wrong. Samuel? Nobody knows about Samuel; I've been too careful. Now I look at him, and his next four words are like a foreign language I can't decode.

"I found the letter."

When his meaning sinks in, the shock is like a wallop to my chest. I yank my hands away and grab my backpack. I check the zip pocket, my heart banging so hard I think it's going to punch through my ribs. The pocket is empty. I feel sick.

"Lauren, it's not there."

I keep looking through the rest of the bag, my hands wild things, tearing through suntan lotion, sunhats ... where is it? I reach the bottom, madly scratching around. There's no crinkle of envelope.

Harry touches my shoulder. "Lauren, stop. I left it in the cabin. In your bedside drawer. It's okay. It's alright."

"It's not! Why did you? How could you?"

"It was on the floor, with your other junk," he says. "I couldn't help but see who it was from. And I wondered why you would carry it around with you after all this time. And then it twigged. It was him, wasn't it? He was the real reason you left."

"No!" I'm not hearing this. I put my hands over my ears and scream it at him. "That was mine. It was for me. He wrote it for me. How could you go through my stuff? I NEVER went through your stuff while you away. Do you know that? I never pried, never broke your trust."

"I didn't ..." Harry is panicking, trying to draw me into his arms. "Shhh."

I lash out, shove him away. "Don't you tell me to shush. Get off!"

"Lauren, stop it. Calm down."

"I won't! You ... you ... I should have known better than to trust you."

I'm too angry to cry. Something small and hard buried inside me has come back to life. It's swelling, putrid and ugly. I should be over this. God. Why won't it leave me alone? I scrabble to my feet. "Fuck you, Harry."

I tear back down the path, slipping on rocks, crying out, branches whipping my legs and arms, until I bump into Luke at the bottom.

"We're going," I tell him, and climb into the back of his car.

Harry isn't far behind me, and when he climbs in, I hold up a hand without looking at him. "Don't even."

Back at the ship, he has the decency to let me head back to our cabin alone. It's only when I'm sitting on my bunk, still furious, that I open my drawer and pull out the scrunched letter. And realise it's still sealed.

23

Nadir

Our room is a frigid wasteland. Harry has given up trying to talk to me. I don't blame him. I'm an iceberg in tropical waters, unable to melt. On stage you'd never know anything was wrong, we smile, we perform, we party. Then the switch flips, and it's arctic. Just as well we've only got another couple of days before we can go back to our own lives.

I'm broken.

We're broken.

Our relationship is a rusty wreck, abandoned and sinking at sea. Nothing is going to mend this.

24

Dissolution

Our plane has landed, and again I have to give Harry credit. He hasn't even tried to make small talk, apart from necessary exchanges. Probably because I've mastered a flat tone to my voice that's an un-scalable wall. He may as well be sitting next to a stranger, the kind that makes you want to bury your face in a book so you don't have to interact with them.

He's tense. I can see it. Feel it. Finally, he breaks his silence.

"What's the plan?"

I shrug.

"Are we calling it quits or what?"

You'd think I'd have that answer at the ready. I've had days to agonise over it, but the decision has eluded me. Obviously, I'll be moving back to my and Snap's apartment, but what happens then? Is the music over? I guess it has to be. We can't continue like this, not that I'm angry anymore. What I am is lost. Back at sea. The one we just left.

"Is that what you want?" I ask, afraid to look at him.

"Is it what you want?"

I can't answer. I honestly don't think it's possible to fix this. Trust is like a broken cup: you can glue it back together, but there's always going to be that worry in the back of your mind that one day it'll leak or fall apart, and you'll get scalded.

"Suit yourself," Harry says, pulling my bag from the overhead locker and dumping it on the seat beside me. "Let me know when you get over yourself."

I bite my lip through the sting of his words. "I'll get a taxi and text you when I get home. I'll have to borrow Snap's car to get my stuff."

"Don't be stupid. I'll drive you."

I shrug again. Am I the arsehole?

It's getting dark and raining heavily when we emerge from the terminal. Cars whoosh, announcements echo, security officers yell at people for parking where they shouldn't. I pull my jacket close as we line up for a taxi. When it comes, the driver is one of those chatty types. He wants to know where we've been, what we've been doing. Harry keeps him happy with glossed-over snippets of what it's like working on a cruise. It staggers me how he sounds so casual. I'm counting the minutes until I can curl up with a hot chocolate in my own bed. If I still have one. Maybe it'll be the couch.

Winter has taken root in Harry's apartment. While we were away, it insinuated itself into the fabrics and furnishings, the walls even. Icy. I go straight to my room. My room. How odd that sounds now. I open my suitcase and start stuffing in as much as I can. Where am I going to get boxes for the other stuff? I'll have to ask Harry to lend me his suitcase. I turn to find him standing in the doorway watching.

He looks weary, his hair hanging in his eyes, hands shoved in pockets, shoulder leaning against the door. How is it he still manages to cut through to my heart?

"You can leave it until morning, you know," he says. "It's late. It's pouring out there. One more night won't make any difference."

I'm torn, bone weary and hungry. I suppose he's right. I just don't want to drag out the torment.

"Stay," he says. "I'll order pizza."

I'm too drained to argue. "Okay."

He leaves me, and I sit on the bed, wishing Mr Pink were here to cuddle. He probably thinks we've deserted him. I get up again and continue to sort things into piles, trying to figure if I can fit everything into two suitcases. When I can't do any more, I sit and wonder. What now? Tomorrow I'll be back to "normal", whatever that is.

The doorbell rings, and Harry fetches the pizza. Eventually, I wander into the kitchen. He holds up a bottle of champagne, looks at me questioningly. "May as well use it, hey?"

I'm surprised he's offering me alcohol after all that's happened. "Sure. Why not? We can toast our demise." My laugh is forced.

Harry doesn't smile, just hands me a glass and holds his out. "Truce," he says.

"Truce."

It's hard to eat pizza when you're sad. Deeply, cruelly, incurably sad. It sticks to your throat and sits like a heavy lump in your stomach. Harry watches me refill my glass but doesn't say anything. Am I going to feel guilty every time I have a drink in front of him? Then again, maybe there won't be any more times.

He clears his throat. "So, listen. I just want to say one thing."

I wait, biting my knuckle.

"I want to apologise. I should have been more supportive ... about that guy touching you. You were right; he was out of order. I should have understood. I was just thinking about not losing our jobs. I didn't get it, and ... I'm really sorry."

I take a shuddering breath, clinch my fingers on my glass as I focus on the champagne bubbles rising in narrow columns, then whisper the first honest thing I've said in weeks. "I tried to stop him."

"I know. If I'd seen it happen, maybe—"

"No. I mean Samuel."

Snap is blooming. He grabs me in a bear hug before I'm inside the door. "OMG, girl, how are you? Thank god you're back. I've put on ten kilos since Granny's been cooking for me, and she piled lashings of food in the freezer before she left. If I start wearing stretchy pants, kill me, will you?"

I wrestle myself free. "OMG yourself, your slur is nearly gone. And look at your face! It's nearly back to normal."

"I knooow right? A miracle, isn't it? Granny helped. Pushed me every day with the speech therapy."

He helps me carry my cases to my bedroom. I look around. Everything is neat. Snap nudges me with his hip. "So, where's that man of yours? Not stopping to say hello?"

"No. He's got stuff to do."

Snap tries to examine my face, but I turn away. "Come here," he says, hugging me again. "You're so skinny! What have they been doing to you?"

"Nothing. I'm fine." I grin to prove it.

He calls my bluff. "So," he says, "Trouble in paradise." He's savvy enough not to push me, "Okay, well what do you want to do?"

"Let's talk about you. What about your man? The flower pot guy? Ben, yeah?"

He rolls his eyes in delight, claps his hands like a happy child. "Now there's a subject I never get tired of. Follow me, I want you to meet someone."

He spins and heads towards his closed bedroom door. Oh geez, please tell me he's not here. I'm not ready for meeting boyfriends. I close my eyes, do the deep breath thing, then plod on behind him. I can do this. It's Snap. I've got to be happy for him.

He turns the doorhandle, cooing. "Here, sweetie. Daddy's here. I want you to meet someone special."

God save me. Is that how he talks to his boyfriend? He gently pushes the door open, and a little black nose appears in the gap, then a long, shiny brown face attached to a wiggly body comes tearing out. It's a sausage dog!

"Meet Charlie."

Snap's face sparkles as he sits in his favourite chair while Charlie tries to lick his face off. While he half-heartedly fights off his fur-buddy, he tells me how Ben and Granny have turned him around. Granny is no nonsense, and Ben – the donor of this blessed little munchkin – is sweet, attentive and a rock for his creative soul. I listen and smile where it's appropriate, giving words of encouragement. I'm happy for him, but some tiny, ugly part of me is resentful. Which is disgusting, because Snap is my best friend, and no way would I want to go through what he's been through. Still, I wonder. Have I been replaced?

"Umm, I think I'll take nap. I'm falling asleep here."

"Kitten, it's only eleven, and I've got morning tea ready."

"Just give me an hour. I'm beat."

It's hard to be sad when you're woken up by a doggy face wash. I push Charlie and his pink tongue away. "Thanks, matey." He sits back and waits. If sugar could be moulded into something brown-furred and wiggly-tailed, this is what it would look like. So smooth and silky soft. I can see why Snap fell for him: those big, shiny trusting eyes daring you not to love him.

Snap's in the kitchen pottering. The sound of contentment. I sag, knowing we're going to have to have "the conversation". But this won't be so bad. It helped opening the wound last night. Now it needs to drain. I can do this. Charlie agrees, his whole bottom wiggling in affirmation. God, he's cute.

Snap's prepared a feast to "put some meat on my skinny bones". The coffee from his new espresso machine is good and hot, liquid gold. We sit opposite each other at the kitchen counter, Charlie at Snap's feet ready to catch anything he might not-so-accidentally drop. We glance at each other between mouthfuls, exchanging smiles. It's good to be back.

"So?" he says.

I put my fork down and slowly finish chewing my smoked salmon and benny egg on an English muffin.

I swallow, look up at him. "I fucked up."

25

Ingress

There's rain spattering the dust on the windshield, and Jack Johnson is on the radio, singing "Better Together". I think he's right. Harry takes one hand off the steering wheel and squeezes my knee. "Hang in there." I wish I could take his comfort, suck it down inside me and use it to quell my simmering nausea.

I look back to Snap who's fallen asleep on the rear seat with Charlie on his lap. His head lolls to one side and a string of dribble is suspended from the weak side of his mouth. I resist a motherly urge to reach back and wipe it away for him. Let him rest. What he doesn't know won't hurt him. Instead, I lower my window and let the wind cool my face.

Mum's dead. The words keep circulating, trying to find a place to land, to take root and become something real in my mind. Dead. Dead. Dead. I'm officially an orphan.

Jack's song finishes as we pull up outside a milk bar in some town I haven't noticed the name of. It's Sunday afternoon, and the shopping strip looks deserted. Harry picks up his wallet from the console. "Thirsty?"

I nod.

"Maybe some Lucozade or something? You're looking peaky. Still not hungry?"

I mumble negatives and shake my head. When did I last eat? Lunch yesterday? Probably. My stomach has been a clenched fist since Harry turned up on our doorstep. I thought I'd forgotten something at his apartment, and he was returning it. That was until I saw his face. And his words made everything spin in my head.

Harry gets out the car. "Leave it with me."

The slamming of his door jars. Every noise, every sensation, feels amplified. I should offer to drive some, but my limbs are leaden from lack of sleep. Or fear. I rest my head against the window.

Next to the milk bar is one of those old-fashioned hardware-gift stores with handyman tools in one window, and homey gifts like candles, tea towels and kitsch plastic trays in the other. Maybe I should get some plastic flowers for Samuel's grave. You're welcome, arsehole.

Something catches my eye: a crow settling on the edge of a garbage bin. Its spidery claws clutch the rim as it pokes through the rubbish. It stops and tilts its head, one shiny eye glaring at me. I know what you're doing, it seems to say. Crows. With their oily feathered bodies. Aren't they harbingers of bad news? Bad omens? He's a bit late.

I think I'm going to be sick. I push my door open. The crow flutters, then resettles. I swing my legs out and rest my elbows on my knees, head down. I've got nothing left to purge. Why won't the nausea go away? I breathe deeply and let the air out slowly. Again. It helps. I pull my legs back in and relax into my seat. My movements have disturbed the crow again, but it continues to perch warily.

I close my eyes and think of what's ahead. What will I say? What exact words will I use? Maybe something short, sharp and subtle that causes confusion and a realisation that this is not a homecoming. That this is not a prodigal daughter come to speak at her mother's funeral. Or shall I go for the jugular and tell them all how it really was?

I picture myself walking up the aisle, standing at the lectern, facing the congregation. I speak slowly, clearly. "Let me tell you a story."

Exactly, the crow says. Tell it exactly like it is.

I open my eyes and stare back at it. "I will."

And then what?

"What do you mean?"

Nothing will have changed. He'll still be who he was. You'll still be who you are.

"No. You're wrong."

Am I?

I want to knock it off its perch. What does it know? And then I remind myself this is Mum's funeral. Not Samuel's.

Harry opens his door, startling me, and drops heavily into his seat. "Here." He passes me a bottle of lemonade and a chocolate frog with hundreds and thousands on it.

"Thanks."

"Who're you talking to?" he asks.

"No-one. Myself." I slam my door, and the crow takes flight. I close my eyes, trying to ease the nausea.

Harry's Coke bottle fizzes as he twists the cap. He gulps a few times, then quietly burps. Polite.

"You know we can turn back?" Harry says. "Anytime you want."

"Yeah. I know," I say, eyes still closed.

He's watching me. I can feel it. Can picture the concern on his face. He knows me now. Knows it all. I owed him that much. I hated seeing the pain on his face, but he told me he needed to hear it. He's something, is Harry. Doesn't have to be here, but his presence is all that's keeping me together.

He taps my arm. "Drink something at least. Get some liquid and sugar into you. You'll feel better."

"Okay."

I force a few sips of lemonade down, and he's right: once the sugar fuels me, the nausea eases. Snap has woken with the door slam. Harry hands him a drink and a packet of chips. I don't have to turn to know that little Charlie is all expectant eyes and open mouth. Are you going to eat that? I smile for the first time in hours.

Another hour on, and we're into Mallee country. Endless fields of wheat and barley-sown fields struggling through a dry winter. The few drops that do fall are lucky to penetrate the crust of the topsoil. The farmers will be doing it tough again.

Rihanna's "Umbrella" comes on the radio. The whine in her voice grates on me. No, you can't be my umbrella. I need to feel the rain.

Mary's porch. You'd think I've come back from the dead the way she grabs and holds me tight. "Oh, my girl. Oh, my girl." It's all she can get out.

"Don't cry," I mumble, trying hard to take my own advice, sinking into her familiar bulky softness. She's still wearing that old apron with its stupid-coloured fruit and leaves.

Fred is hanging around in the background, shuffling, hands in pockets. When Mary lets me go, I give him a kiss on the cheek. "Good to see you," he says.

I step back to let Harry greet his grandparents. Snap is still back at the car, putting a lead on Charlie. He stands and squints across the road to the remains of Samuel's house. I turn away. I don't want to see it. Not yet.

Mary ushers us inside to a Christmas-like spread on her dining table. I smile. Feeding people is what she knows. She questions us on where we've been, what we've been up to.

"I was so glad to hear you're both making a go of music." She winks. "I always hoped you two would end up together."

Harry and I exchange looks. I shove a big piece of ham in my mouth, appetite suddenly returned. Actually being here doesn't seem as bad as the thought of being here. What was I so worried about? I'm surrounded by people who love me.

Snap asks Mary about a recipe for her lamb cutlets. After we've all had a giant slice of Mary's cream sponge, topped with ridiculous amounts of homemade strawberry jam, the conversation turns to the funeral.

"I hope Wednesday suits you all?" says Mary. "I figured you'd want a couple of days to think about who you want there, who you want to speak, flowers, all that sort of thing?"

"It's fine," I say, wishing it was actually today so we could get it over with.

"I wasn't sure if you wanted an open casket, that sort of thing."

I breathe out. "No. I don't think so."

"Whatever you want, sweetheart. She was your mum, after all."

I niggle at this. I know she was my mum. I don't need to be reminded. Guilt. Mary is just trying to make things easy for me.

The guys retreat to the lounge while Mary and I head to the kitchen. Her odd fruity apron doesn't annoy me anymore. She hands me another, one with rosebuds on it, and we stand side by side at the sink, me washing, her drying. The afternoon sun is streaming through the window, and the backyard looks exactly the way it did when I left. I'm surprised a dog named Toto isn't sitting at my feet.

Mary doesn't say anything when one of my tears falls into the dishwater, or when I finally tell her about Samuel. She just listens, like she knew all along. And it makes me wonder why I thought it would be so hard. And I wonder too, what will happen to the dead space inside me, now that I've let the air in.

"I'm here," Mary says.

What is it with older women being mind-readers? She tells me to take care of myself because sometimes these things have a way of sneaking up on you when you're not expecting it, that there's no shame in asking for help – professional help, that I might still have sad moments, scared moments, but to pick up the phone when that happens. No matter where or when. Always.

"God," I say. "I feel like I've been angry my whole life."

Harry and I sit on Mary's front porch. The funeral was exhausting, but good, as funerals go, I guess. Snap is in the kitchen with Mary, trying to steal some more recipes. I keep glancing across the road.

"Time for a stroll?" Harry asks.

"Maybe."

We sit a while longer, watching a couple of noisy miner birds scratching underneath a straggly lavender shrub. Slim pickings. Along Mary's fence line, orange rosehips, like spherical lollipops, cling to the ends of dead-looking branches. The chill of the wind is familiar here, but the anger and disillusionment have slipped away. Coming back isn't what I thought it would be; I'm not sure what I was expecting – a confrontation? With whom?

So much time wasted. I have to start putting things right in my life. I look at Harry in his cosy wool jacket, his five o'clock shadow darkening his chin.

"I've been trying to sort my head out," I say.

Harry nods. "Hmm."

"Harry?" He turns to me. "I want you to know that I'm grateful for all you've done."

He smiles, takes my hand. His face is so open, concerned, so beautiful.

I know what I want now. But I struggle to get my voice out. "This music thing. What if it's over?"

Harry looks away. He doesn't want to hear. But he has to.

"I'm not sure I have what it takes."

He shakes his head. "Don't say that. You've got more talent—"

"It's not enough."

"But—"

"Shhh. Let me finish. Yes, a good voice, but I don't have a fire inside me, and it shows. Yes, I love to sing ... but I'm scared of putting myself out there. It hurts. At least ... at the moment."

I wait. There's a muscle twitching in his jaw. His eyes are focused straight ahead.

"You could learn."

I sigh. "I have other things I need to learn first. But you. You're the one with real talent. I've always said that. You have to keep going. Keep writing. Finish your degree."

"Uh huh."

"And Harry?"

He won't look at me. His face is set. Steely. I bite down on my lip. "Okay," I say. "Let's take that walk?"

He doesn't say anything, but he stands, still holding my hand, tighter. We walk down the steps, through the garden and head out the gate.

Samuel's place. I can see from here that there's not much left. Mary said most of the wreckage was cleared – a danger for inquisitive kids. As we get closer, I keep my eyes on the road, the loose gravel at its edges, the dandelions in the nature strip, the footpath, until we reach the gate. I look up. Another false expectation: I thought the ground would still be blackened from the fire, but seasons and nature have rubbed away the ashes. A few scorched bricks, the cement steps, bits of unrecognisable rubble sit in the red dirt.

I lean on the fence, taking in the debris of my past.

"Okay?" Harry asks.

"Yep."

I'd always pictured myself hyperventilating at this point. I'm not. I open the creaky gate. Push through. Past the remnants of foundations, Mum's cement tubs. I point. "Mum's swing chair was there. We spent hours watching the stars."

Down by the back fence, the fruit trees have survived. They're all winter-bare except for the lemon tree. It's flourishing, white sweet-scented blossoms unfurling and a few fallen fruits at its base. I wouldn't be surprised if Mary's been watering it – it's the only piece of yard with a decent patch of grass. We head over and sit beneath it.

"There's nothing left," I murmur.

"Well, you did a bloody good job," he says.

"What?" I look at him, shocked, then laugh. And we laugh together until my stomach hurts and tears run.

"I'm sorry," he says.

"For what?"

"For ... everything. For this. For you. For us. For what he did to you."

I nod. "Me too."

I tug up a bit of couch grass and rub it between my fingers. "He was all I had left, with you gone, Mum gone ... well, her mind, at least. I trusted him. I think that's what I don't know if I can forgive. The trust."

Harry's knee is resting against mine. I like it there. He puts an arm around me, and I lean back into him. It's nice. A sad nice.

"It's funny," I say. "As much as I've tried not to think about it, to block it out, there's something I remember. When Samuel was ... on top of me, I could see the mantelpiece, and there was Mum's ceramic vase with its little cherubs on either side. It had a crack running up its centre from when I'd knocked it over as a kid. Dad glued it back together. I don't know why I noticed it. Maybe it was the glow from Samuel's digital clock. And ... well ... the cherubs on the vase were smiling down at me, as if to say it doesn't matter, we all get broken at some point."

Harry's quiet. He doesn't know what to say.

"Are we broken?" I ask.

"I'm not sure," he says slowly.

"Do you think we could find some glue to fix us? Put us back together like Humpty Dumpty?"

"They couldn't put Humpty back together again."

"Bad analogy."

"Very."

We're quiet for a while. A beetle appears near my foot, struggling through the blades of grass.

Harry shifts. "I'm confused. I thought you didn't want ... us."

I turn to him. "Us? No, no, not us. It's the music I don't think I can do. I want us. I just ... wasn't sure if you wanted us... without the music."

"Oh."

I can look him in the eye now. Now that he knows everything. Everything. He seems older than back in February when he grinned at me in Bob's bar. Did I do that? Is that what love does to people?

I speak slowly, clearly. "I. Want. Us."

He nods, leans in. And here is the kiss. The one that feels like home. The one that makes me want to fold myself up into something tiny and hop into his shirt pocket so he can carry me around near his heart always.

He pulls back, and there it is at last — I'm the girl who makes him smile.

"There's one more thing," I say, then lean forward and reach into my back pocket. Samuel's letter. I hold it in my lap, looking at the worn envelope. Déjà vu.

"It's lost its power," I murmur. "I can't believe it. I've been letting this stupid piece of paper hold me hostage. I thought as long as I didn't open it, I was the one with the power. Because he couldn't say sorry."

"Are you going to read it now?"

"I don't know. What's the point? Nothing will change if I do."

"Maybe. Maybe not. I still think you should."

I sniff. "I noticed there's a new plaque outside the post office. It's dedicated to Samuel."

"Yeah? How do you feel about that?"

"Spell ambivalent."

He squeezes me. "You're allowed to say it sucks."

"Okay. It sucks."

He chuckles.

I say it louder. "It sucks. SUCKS!"

"Feel better?"

"Not really."

I stand up and reach into my other pocket.

"What are you doing?"

"Finishing this." I show him the lighter.

"Oh shit." Harry scrambles to his feet and backs off, but he's laughing. "Let me get a safe distance."

I straighten out the envelope and flick the lighter. The paper catches and flares.

"Samuel Barnes," I yell. "You lonely, sad, drunk, pathetic man. I forgive you. You hear me? I don't care what your letter says. I forgive you. Not for you. For me."

I hold the burning envelope, charred pieces fluttering, becoming airborne, ashes rising, then floating back to earth.

I'm not stupid. I'm aware forgiveness isn't that simple. It will ebb and flow. Maybe there'll be times when I'll regret this ... this letting go. Times when I'll want to claw back my anger. Those times will pass. Right now, I need this unburdening.

Soon the flame is reaching my fingers, so I drop the remainder on the grass and glance up at the lemon tree. I choose a large, juicy fruit and snap it off its branch. I dig a hole in the peel, then squeeze juice over the smouldering cinders.

"What are you doing?"

Samuel would get it. "Spell congruous."

My beautiful, beautiful girl

What have I done?

Damaged you beyond

Repair and now I leave

The coward that I am

Forgive me.

An easy way to support your favourite authors

Did you know that leaving a review on Goodreads or Amazon will make you 10% more attractive? It's also one of the quickest and easiest ways to show your support for an author. A single sentence from you (it doesn't need to be an essay) helps authors be seen by other readers.
So while you're here, why don't you pop onto one of the sites now and leave a quick review? I would be super grateful you made the effort.

Acknowledgements

Chris Collins, Kathryn Moore, Jo Burnell, Connie Spanos, Nicole Hayes, Melissa Manning, Nikki Bielinski, Sylvia Goudie, Adam VanLangenberg, Tim Byrne, Deborah Vanderwerp, Hutch Stevens, Ari Gershevitch, Geraldine Stallard, Andrew Pelechaty, Ruth Van Gramberg, Sally Odgers, Theresa Bonn, Lana Collins, Joe Pryke, my RMIT tutors and fellow students.

Each of you have accompanied me along this bumpy ride, helping me develop as an author and a better person with your patience, generosity and skill. Thank you. No author does it alone, and you were the best literary companions a person could ask for.

About the author

Cienna Collins is an Australian author of domestic noir suspense. Her books were longlisted for the QWC Adaptable film and television program and won a Publishable mentorship. Cienna was also awarded a placement at Hardcopy – a national professional development program for writers. Her short stories have won numerous awards and have been read on Radio Queensland.

Cienna has an Associate Degree in Professional Writing & Editing and runs a successful book editing and audiobook production business, AJC Publishing. Previous to this, Cienna had an eclectic career including managing commercial mortgages, working in a legal tribunal and fronting her own function band for over twenty years.

A previous devotee of adrenaline sports, including bungee jumping, skydiving, parasailing, sky-walking, sky-jumping and volcano climbing, Cienna is now happy to be settled at home in Melbourne with her hubby and two fur-kids, writing her adventures instead of living dangerously.

Stay in Touch
Join Cienna's mailing list: https://ciennacollins.com

www.ingramcontent.com/pod-product-compliance
Lightning Source LLC
Chambersburg PA
CBHW030548080526
44585CB00012B/299